WISE SAYINGS

from

PROVERBS

WISE SAYINGS

from

PROVERBS

LION

Compiled by Olivia Warburton
This edition copyright © 2011 Lion Hudson
The author asserts the moral right
to be identified as the author of this work

A Lion Book
an imprint of
Lion Hudson plc
Wilkinson House, Jordan Hill Road,
Oxford OX2 8DR, England
www.lionhudson.com
ISBN 978 0 7459 5553 7

Distributed by:
UK: Marston Book Services, PO Box 269,
Abingdon, Oxon, OX14 4YN
USA: Trafalgar Square Publishing, 814 N.
Franklin Street, Chicago, IL 60610
USA Christian Market: Kregel Publications,
PO Box 2607, Grand Rapids, MI 49501

First edition 2011
10 9 8 7 6 5 4 3 2 1 0
All rights reserved

Acknowledgments
pp. 14t, 20b, 34t, 38, 42b, 45, 48b, 52b, 55b,
58m: Scripture quotations are from *The Holy
Bible, English Standard Version*, published by
HarperCollins Publishers, copyright © 2001
Crossway Bibles, a division of Good News
Publishers. Used by permission. All rights
reserved. pp. 23t, 24t, 30b, 32b, 35t, 36t,
42t, 47t, 49, 56t: Scripture quotations are
from the *Good News Bible* published by the
Bible Societies and HarperCollins Publishers,
© American Bible Society 1994, used with
permission. pp. 12, 14b, 15b, 21, 22, 26, 31t,
32t, 34b, 35b, 36m, 43b, 51, 55t, 56b, 58b:
Scripture quotations taken from the *Holy Bible,
New International Version*, copyright © 1973,
1978, 1984 International Bible Society. Used
by permission of Zondervan and Hodder
& Stoughton Limited. All rights reserved.
The 'NIV' and 'New International Version'
trademarks are registered in the United States
Patent and Trademark Office by International
Bible Society. Use of either trademark
requires the permission of International
Bible Society. UK trademark number 1448790.

pp. 13, 15t, 16, 25, 30t, 33, 37, 44, 46t, 48t:
The New King James Version copyright © 1982,
1979 by Thomas Nelson, Inc. J.B. Phillips
Reprinted with the permission of Simon &
Schuster from *The New Testament in Modern
English, Revised Edition*, translated by
J. B. Phillips. Copyright © 1958, 1960, 1972
by J. B. Phillips. Reprinted from *The New
Testament in Modern English, Revised Edition*,
translated by J.B. Phillips. Published by
HarperCollins Publishers Ltd. pp. 6, 10,
11, 20t, 24b, 31b, 47b, 53t, 54t, 57t, 58t:
Scripture quotations are taken from the *Holy
Bible, New Living Translation*, copyright ©
1996. Used by permission of Tyndale House
Publishers, Inc., Wheaton, Illinois 60189.
All rights reserved. pp. 23b, 27, 36b, 39, 43t,
46b, 53b, 54b, 57b, 59: Scripture quotations
are from the *New Revised Standard Version*
published by HarperCollins Publishers,
copyright © 1989 by the Division of Christian
Education of the National Council of the
Churches of Christ in the USA, and are used
by permission.
All rights reserved.

A catalogue record for this book is available
from the British Library
Typeset in 10.5/12 Perpetua and 10/24
Zapfino
Printed and bound in China

ONTENTS

INTRODUCTION

Throughout the ages the Proverbs have been celebrated for their spiritual insight and ability to speak to the heart of the human condition.

This collection brings together passages from this unique work of wisdom literature. By exploring a range of issues – whether justice or simple living, decision-making or how to know God – and contrasting right with wrong, these ancient writings point us towards the best way to shape our lives.

How much better to get wisdom than gold, and good judgment than silver!

PROVERBS 16:16

WISDOM

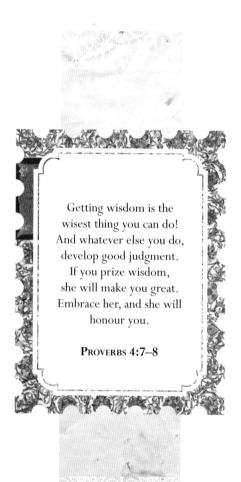

Getting wisdom is the
wisest thing you can do!
And whatever else you do,
develop good judgment.
If you prize wisdom,
she will make you great.
Embrace her, and she will
honour you.

PROVERBS 4:7–8

My child, listen to what I say,
and treasure my commands.
Tune your ears to wisdom,
and concentrate on understanding.
Cry out for insight,
and ask for understanding.
Search for them as you would for silver;
seek them like hidden treasures.
Then you will understand what
it means to fear the Lord,
and you will gain knowledge of God.
For the Lord grants wisdom!
From his mouth come knowledge and understanding.
He grants a treasure of common sense to the honest.
He is a shield to those who walk with integrity.
He guards the paths of the just
and protects those who are faithful to him.

PROVERBS 2:1–8

Wisdom has built her house;
she has set up its seven pillars.
She has prepared her meat
and mixed her wine;
she has also set her table.
She has sent out her servants, and she calls
from the highest point of the city,
"Let all who are simple come to my house!"
To those who have no sense she says,
"Come, eat my food
and drink the wine I have mixed.
Leave your simple ways and you will live;
walk in the way of insight."

PROVERBS 9:1–6

Through wisdom
a house is built,
And by understanding
it is established;
By knowledge
the rooms are filled
With all precious
and pleasant riches.

PROVERBS 24:3–4

13

Listen to advice and accept instruction,
that you may gain wisdom in the future.

PROVERBS 19:20

*Start children off
on the way they should go,
and even when they are old
they will not turn from it.*

PROVERBS 22:6

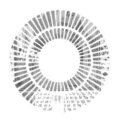

He who earnestly seeks
good finds favour,
But trouble will come
to him who seeks evil.

PROVERBS 11:27

The one who has knowledge uses words with restraint,
and whoever has understanding is even-tempered.
Even fools are thought wise if they keep silent,
and discerning if they hold their tongues.

PROVERBS 17:27–28

Happy is the man who finds wisdom,
And the man who gains understanding;
For her proceeds are better than the profits of silver,
And her gain than fine gold.
She is more precious than rubies,
And all the things you may desire
cannot compare with her.
Length of days is in her right hand,
In her left hand riches and honour.
Her ways are ways of pleasantness,
And all her paths are peace.
She is a tree of life to those who take hold of her,
And happy are all who retain her.

PROVERBS 3:13–18

fine gold

INTEGRITY

The way of the righteous is like the first gleam of dawn,
which shines ever brighter until the full light of day.

PROVERBS 4:18

Whoever walks in integrity
walks securely,
but he who makes his ways
crooked will be found out.

PROVERBS 10:9

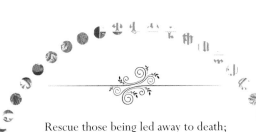

Rescue those being led away to death;
hold back those staggering toward slaughter.
If you say, "But we knew nothing about this,"
does not he who weighs the heart perceive it?
Does not he who guards your life know it?
Will he not repay each person according
to what he has done?

PROVERBS 24:11–12

There are six things the Lord hates,
seven that are detestable to him:
haughty eyes,
a lying tongue,
hands that shed innocent blood,
a heart that devises wicked schemes,
feet that are quick to rush into evil,
a false witness who pours out lies
and a person who stirs up conflict in
the community.

PROVERBS 6:16–19

Do what is right and fair;
that pleases the Lord more
than bringing him sacrifices.

PROVERBS 21:3

Speak out for those who cannot speak,
for the rights of all the destitute.
Speak out, judge righteously,
defend the rights of the poor and needy.

PROVERBS 31:8–9

23

If you oppress poor people,
you insult the God who made them;
but kindness shown to the poor
is an act of worship.

PROVERBS 14:31

Those who shut their ears
to the cries of the poor will be ignored
in their own time of need.

PROVERBS 21:13

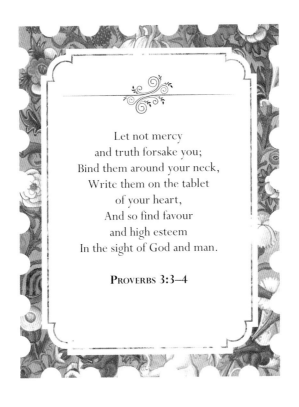

Let not mercy
and truth forsake you;
Bind them around your neck,
Write them on the tablet
of your heart,
And so find favour
and high esteem
In the sight of God and man.

PROVERBS 3:3–4

All a person's ways seem pure to them,
but motives are weighed by the Lord.

PROVERBS 16:2

No one can be established
through wickedness,
but the righteous cannot
be uprooted.

PROVERBS 12:3

springs of

Keep your heart with all vigilance,
for from it flow the springs of life.

PROVERBS 4:23

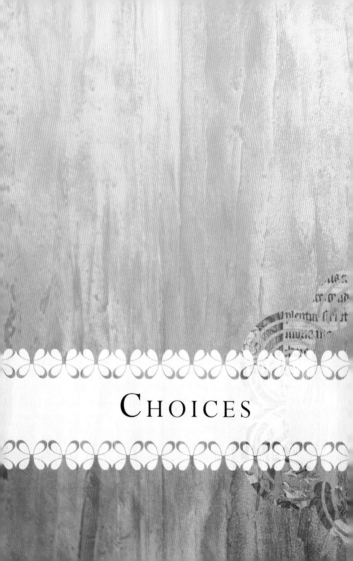

CHOICES

If your enemy is hungry, give him bread to eat;
And if he is thirsty, give him water to drink;
For so you will heap coals of fire on his head,
And the Lord will reward you.

PROVERBS 25:21–22

*Don't be glad when your
enemies meet disaster,
and don't rejoice when
they stumble.*

PROVERBS 24:17

Do not withhold good from those to whom it is due,
when it is in your power to act.
Do not say to your neighbour,
"Come back tomorrow and I'll give it to you" –
when you already have it with you.

PROVERBS 3:27–28

*A gracious woman gains respect,
but ruthless men gain only wealth.*

PROVERBS 11:16

Starting a quarrel is like breaching a dam;
so drop the matter before a dispute breaks out.

PROVERBS 17:14

Don't take it on yourself
to repay a wrong.
Trust the Lord and he will
make it right.

PROVERBS 20:22

*Whoever digs a pit
will fall into it,
And he who rolls a stone will
have it roll back on him.*

PROVERBS 26:27

Hatred stirs up strife,
But love covers all sins.

PROVERBS 10:12

A man without self-control is like
a city broken into and left without walls.

PROVERBS 25:28

Do not make friends with a hot-tempered person,
do not associate with one easily angered,
or you may learn their ways
and get yourself ensnared.

PROVERBS 22:24–25

A gossip can never keep a secret.
Stay away from people who talk too much.

PROVERBS 20:19

*Like a muddied spring
or a polluted well
are the righteous who give
way to the wicked.*

PROVERBS 25:26

Let other people praise you
— even strangers;
never do it yourself.

PROVERBS 27:2

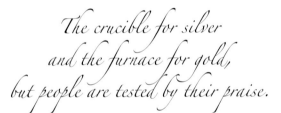

*The crucible for silver
and the furnace for gold,
but people are tested by their praise.*

PROVERBS 27:21

One who gives
an honest answer
gives a kiss on the lips.

PROVERBS 24:26

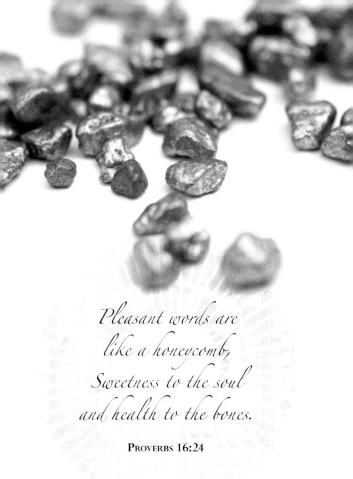

Pleasant words are
like a honeycomb,
Sweetness to the soul
and health to the bones.

PROVERBS 16:24

If one curses his father
or his mother,
his lamp will be put out
in utter darkness.

PROVERBS 20:20

Fools show their anger at once,
but the prudent ignore an insult....
Rash words are like sword thrusts,
but the tongue of the wise
brings healing.

PROVERBS 12:16, 18

MONEY

The rich and the poor have this in common:
the Lord made them both.

PROVERBS 22:2

Two things I ask of you;
deny them not to me before I die:
Remove far from me falsehood and lying;
give me neither poverty nor riches;
feed me with the food that is needful for me,
lest I be full and deny you
and say, "Who is the Lord?"
or lest I be poor and steal
and profane the name of my God.

PROVERBS 30:7–9

Some give freely, yet grow all the richer;
    others withhold what is due,
    and only suffer want.
A generous person will be enriched,
and one who gives water will get water.

PROVERBS 11:24–25

Do not eat the food of a begrudging host,
    do not crave his delicacies;
    for he is the kind of person
who is always thinking about the cost.
"Eat and drink," he says to you,
    but his heart is not with you.

PROVERBS 23:6–7

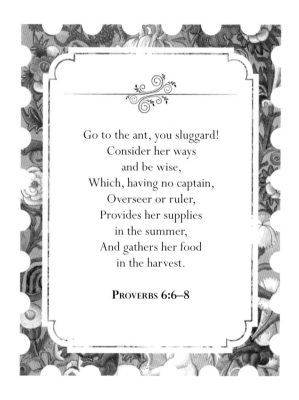

Go to the ant, you sluggard!
Consider her ways
and be wise,
Which, having no captain,
Overseer or ruler,
Provides her supplies
in the summer,
And gathers her food
in the harvest.

PROVERBS 6:6–8

I passed by the field of a sluggard,
by the vineyard of a man lacking sense,
and behold, it was all overgrown with thorns;
the ground was covered with nettles,
and its stone wall was broken down.
Then I saw and considered it;
I looked and received instruction.
A little sleep, a little slumber,
a little folding of the hands to rest,
and poverty will come upon you like a robber,
and want like an armed man.

PROVERBS 24:30–34

*Better is a dry morsel
with quietness,
Than a house full of feasting
with strife.*

PROVERBS 17:1

Do not wear yourself out to get rich;
be wise enough to desist.
When your eyes light upon it, it is gone;
for suddenly it takes wings to itself,
flying like an eagle towards heaven.

PROVERBS 23:4–5

Never boast about tomorrow.
You don't know what will happen
between now and then.

PROVERBS 27:1

Honour the Lord with your wealth
and with the best part of everything you produce.
Then he will fill your barns with grain,
and your vats will overflow with good wine.

PROVERBS 3:9–10

A good name is to be chosen
rather than great riches,
Loving favour rather than
silver and gold.

PROVERBS 22:1

flourish

Whoever trusts in his riches will fall,
but the righteous will flourish like
a green leaf.

PROVERBS 11:28

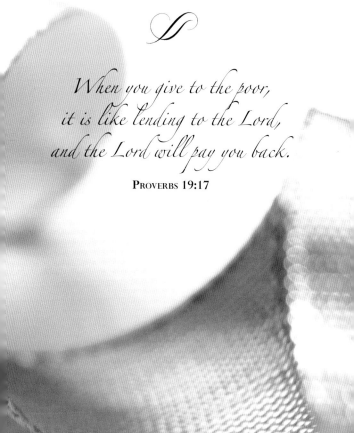

When you give to the poor,
it is like lending to the Lord,
and the Lord will pay you back.

PROVERBS 19:17

SECURITY

Trust in the Lord with all your heart
and lean not on your own understanding;
in all your ways submit to him,
and he will make your paths straight.

PROVERBS 3:5–6

*Commit your work to the Lord,
and your plans will be established.*

PROVERBS 16:3

A cheerful heart is good medicine,
but a broken spirit
saps a person's strength.

PROVERBS 17:22

In the fear of the Lord one has strong confidence,
and one's children will have a refuge.

PROVERBS 14:26

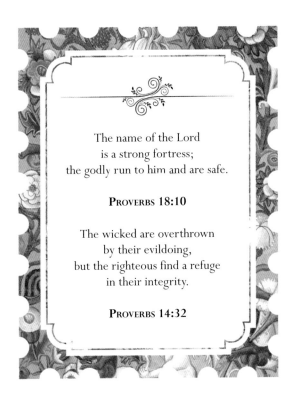

The name of the Lord
is a strong fortress;
the godly run to him and are safe.

PROVERBS 18:10

The wicked are overthrown
by their evildoing,
but the righteous find a refuge
in their integrity.

PROVERBS 14:32

Be sure of this:
The wicked will not
go unpunished,
but those who are righteous
will go free.

PROVERBS 11:21

Pride goes before destruction,
and a haughty spirit before a fall.

PROVERBS 16:18

Can anyone really say
that his conscience is clear,
that he has got rid of his sin?

PROVERBS 20:9

Whoever conceals their sins does not prosper,
but the one who confesses
and renounces them finds mercy.
Blessed is the one who always trembles before God,
but whoever hardens their heart falls into trouble.

PROVERBS 28:13–14

My child, don't reject the Lord's discipline,
and don't be upset when he corrects you.
For the Lord corrects those he loves,
just as a father corrects a child in whom he delights.

PROVERBS 3:11–12

*The crucible is for silver,
and the furnace is for gold,
but the Lord tests the heart.*

PROVERBS 17:3

No human wisdom
or understanding or plan
can stand against the Lord.

PROVERBS 21:30

The fear of the Lord leads to life,
and whoever has It rests satisfied;
he will not be visited by harm.

PROVERBS 19:23

Charm is deceptive,
and beauty is fleeting;
but a woman who fears
the Lord is to be praised.

PROVERBS 31:30

The fear of the Lord is the beginning of wisdom,
and the knowledge of the Holy One is insight.

Proverbs 9:10

fine gold

ACKNOWLEDGMENTS

BACKGROUNDS:
iStock: Jussi Santaniemi

ILLUMINATED MANUSCRIPTS:
Alamy: Classic Image
Corbis: Fine Art Photographic Library; The Gallery Collection

MOTIFS:
iStock: George Peters; iLexx; Jamie Farrant

PHOTOGRAPHS:
Corbis: pp. 6–7 Ingo Boddenberg; pp. 26–27 Ocean; p. 53 moodboard
iStock: pp. 8–9 Andreas Guskos; pp. 18–19 Marcus Lindström; pp. 20, 33, 46 Chris Leachman; pp. 28–29 Larry Cole; p. 39 naqiewei; pp. 40–41 naphtalina; pp. 48–49, 59 DNY59; pp. 50–51 Jane Tyson; p. 52 Laurent Nicod; p. 57 pixhook

COVER
Background: Jussi Santaniemi/iStock
Illuminated manuscript: The Gallery Collection/Corbis
Photograph: Svenja-Foto/Corbis

Charlotte Craven was thankful to be escaping from her recent problems to the magic of the Orient—even if it was a working holiday and her new boss was to be the formidable surgeon Adam Forster, who didn't think much of her or her lack of qualifications. If only she could forget her awful secret . . .

Margaret Barker trained as a State Registered Nurse at a large hospital in the North of England. Soon afterwards, she married a graduate from the nearby university and they have recently celebrated thirty happy years of marriage. They have two sons and a daughter, and one grandchild. Their work has taken them to America, Africa, Asia and Europe, and this has given Margaret ideas for the books which she has set overseas; her own teaching hospital has provided the background for her English stories. She and her husband now live in a sixteenth-century thatched cottage near the sea.

Margaret Barker has written six other Doctor Nurse Romances, the most recent titles being *Olympic Surgeon*, *Love's Cure* and *Dream Doctor*.

HONG KONG SURGEON

BY

MARGARET BARKER

MILLS & BOON LIMITED
15-16 BROOK'S MEWS
LONDON W1A 1DR

*First published in Great Britain 1986
by Mills & Boon Limited*

© Margaret Barker 1986

*Australian copyright 1986
Philippine copyright 1986*

ISBN 0 263 75636 X

*Set in Linotron Times 11 on 11 pt.
03-0187-44985*

*Typeset in Great Britain by
Associated Publishing Services
Printed and bound in Great Britain by
Collins, Glasgow*

CHAPTER ONE

CHARLOTTE gazed down at the blue water of the Bay of Hong Kong. She had never imagined it would be so beautiful. Jane's letters had described the vivid colours of this enchanting island, but she had always thought there was an exaggeration somewhere. Nothing on earth could be so exotic, so lively, so out of this world! She held her breath as the plane swooped down towards the narrow landing strip, skimming dangerously near to the shimmering sea, like some giant primaeval bird. There was a distorted glimpse of the brilliant sails of a sampan before the huge aircraft touched down and hurtled towards the airport amid the cacophony of its thrusting engines.

Phew! Thank goodness for that! For a moment she had thought they weren't going to make it. The doors opened and the hot air poured inside. She would have to go out and face the world again—alone with her awful secret. In some ways it might have been a blessed release if the plane had plunged into the sea. Then she chided herself for being so morbid; life must go on.

She moved through the airport as if in a dream, jostled continually by the excited travellers, anxious to dispense with the boring formalities and escape to the magic of the Orient. Everyone seemed to have someone to meet them. Friendly arms were reaching out in greeting. Cries of 'Over here!', 'Lovely to see you again', mingled with the general noisy confusion and the strange tonal quality of the high-pitched Cantonese voices.

Charlotte stood on the pavement outside, shielding her eyes from the blinding rays of the afternoon sun. Jane had said she would try to meet her if she could, but there was no sign of her. It would have to be a taxi. She moved towards one of the bright red vehicles parked in the roadway.

'I want to go to . . .'

'You must be Charlotte.' A tall, dark stranger placed his hand on her arm. 'Sorry I couldn't get here sooner. Jane will kill me for being late, but I was held up at the hospital. Here, let me take your case. My car's over there.'

'That's very kind of you, Dr Frobisher.'

'Call me Mark, please.' He smiled down at her as he reached for her luggage, and she could see what a handsome husband Jane had. There had been no exaggeration there. She felt as if she had known him for years, but doubted if he would remember her from those far off days at St Catherine's Hospital.

She followed the tall, distinguished figure across the road to a large, luxurious limousine. He was every inch the successful consultant. She thought back to her days as a student nurse when Mark had been a young houseman in love with Jane. It was so romantic that they had met up again and got married after an eight-year separation. Charlotte sighed wistfully. It was like something you read about it a romantic novel. Why didn't things like that happen to her?

Probably because she'd been shut away nursing her sick mother during the time when she should have been out spreading her wings and enjoying herself. And now it was too late; too late at twenty-seven!

'Come round this side, Charlotte.' He was opening the front passenger door for her.

She stepped in as gracefully as possible, but it wasn't something she was used to doing. He caught a glimpse of long slender legs, beneath the frumpy tweed skirt. Pity she dresses like an old woman, he thought. She could look quite attractive in the right clothes, with that tall, skinny figure. Jane warned me that she might have gone to seed, but this is ridiculous! She's the same age as Jane, for God's sake. Poor kid; she's had a hell of a life so far. He climbed in the driver's seat and put the car in gear.

'How did you recognise me?' Charlotte asked guilelessly, scanning the rugged profile at the wheel, with large blue innocent eyes.

He laughed. 'Easy; you've got the same long blonde hair you had when you were eighteen. You haven't changed a bit.'

'So you *do* remember me?'

'Of course I do. How could I forget the times when you used to play gooseberry?'

They both laughed. Mark took his eyes off the road for an instant and thought how much younger she looked when she relaxed. But there was an air of anxiety about her. He would have to get Jane to take her in hand and find out what was the problem. I mean, people don't just ring up out of the blue and say, 'expect me on the next plane—oh, and by the way, can you find me a voluntary nursing job?' he thought.

She looks as if she's running away from something—or somebody, perhaps. True, she's lost both her parents recently, but I would have thought . . .

'It's so colourful!' Charlotte's nose was pressed against the window like a child's as she tried to absorb the kaleidoscope of the narrow street. Overladen stalls encroached over the cobbles, spilling their wares into the dust as the crowds milled around them. Oriental bric-à-brac, Chinese jackets and handbags hung beneath enormous coils of incense which sent out a pall of smoke beneath ancient wooden rafters. And then they were through this memento of a bygone era, back into the twentieth century. Brand new cars jostled for position between trams and bicycles, and designer-style clothes adorned the models in the plate glass windows.

The car ran down through the tunnel beneath the harbour and out on to Hong Kong Island. They were climbing up the road to the Peak. The vast expanse of busy humanity was left far beneath them as Mark turned the car between wrought iron gates and stopped in front of a two-storey Colonial-style building.

'Home at last,' Mark said contentedly, as he climbed out of the car.

'What a lovely house!' Charlotte took in the ornate stone columns on either side of the impressive doorway, the ivy growing up the walls and the huge porcelain vases of tropical plants.

'Charlotte!' A trim, attractive figure was running down the steps towards her.

'Jane!' She was out of the car and running to meet her friend. 'You look marvellous! So this is what motherhood does for you!'

'Did you have a good flight?' Jane linked her arm through Charlotte's and guided her towards the main door.

'Excellent. I've never flown before, you know. I was a bit scared when we took off, but after that . . .'

'Hey, don't I get a welcome?' Mark was still standing in the drive beside the luggage.

Jane laughed and ran back down the steps to kiss her husband. 'I'm sorry, darling, but I haven't see Charlotte for so long. When was the last time?'

'Before you two start trotting down Memory Lane, let me get a word in edgeways; I've got to go back to hospital now. Chien can take the cases inside.'

A white-coated steward had appeared on the steps as he spoke.

'Okay, darling, but don't be long.' Jane smiled lovingly up into Mark's eyes. 'And don't forget to bring Adam with you. He promised to take Charlotte over to Cheung Lau . . .'

'Who's Adam?' asked Charlotte nervously.

A knowing look passed between husband and wife. Mark cleared his throat. 'He's the director of the Cheung Lau project; your new boss.'

'Oh, so you've managed to find me a job. That's wonderful!'

'I should reserve judgement on that till you've talked it over with Adam. There are one or two complications,' Jane said quietly.

'What sort of complications?' Charlotte stared at her friend apprehensively.

Mark was quick to the rescue. 'Nothing we can't handle. Don't worry, Charlotte.'

But she did worry, as she walked into the

cool, elegant interior. Perhaps it had been an imposition to expect Jane to help her. When friends send you an open invitation to visit them, they don't always mean it. And this had been rather a sudden decision.

'You're going to love Hong Kong.' Jane led the way into a bright, airy room flanked on one side with a wide balcony. 'Come and see the view.'

'It's incredible!' Charlotte's fingers tightened automatically on the iron railing, as she stared down at the mind-blowing spectacle. Hong Kong looked like an exotic toy-town, made up of every colour of the rainbow. Tiny vehicles mingled with tall skyscraper buildings, and further away on the blue harbour, the fishing boats, sampans and ocean-going vessels cruised along, easily, like coloured beetles on a smooth, unruffled millpond.

'I love living out here,' Jane said happily. 'But what about you? Why the impetuous rush out here? Not that I'm not delighted to see you, of course,' she added hastily.

'I had to get away. Everything was crowding in on me. It's all been too much, and now . . .' Charlotte stopped, as she choked back the tears.

'Don't talk about it, if it upsets you. Come and sit down. Chien will bring us some tea.' Jane's arm was round her friend's shoulders as she rang a bell. 'You've had an awful time, I know. Your letters were always cheerful, but, reading between the lines, it must have been hell.'

'It was,' said Charlotte tonelessly.

'It must have been such a shock when your

father had that heart attack, so soon after your mother's funeral.'

'Daddy had always managed to keep going, when Mummy was ill. He never complained, just got on with the endless work in the surgery and went out on his rounds. I used to help out when Mummy didn't need me, but I think he pushed himself to the limit.'

'How's your little sister?' asked Jane.

'Julia? She's not so little now; takes her finals at the end of the year.'

'Really? How time flies!' Jane paused and took a deep breath. 'So why the sudden change of plan? One minute you're vaguely promising to come out in a few months and the next you're on the phone . . .'

'Please, don't ask any more questions; there is a reason, but it's something I have to come to terms with. I don't want to discuss it.'

'I'm sorry; I didn't mean to pry,' Jane said hastily. 'Here's the tea. Thank you, Chien; you can put it down on this table. Do you still take sugar, Charlotte?' She busied herself with the cups and saucers. Whatever it was that was worrying her friend would probably sort itself out while she was over here. There was nothing like a change of scene for helping to put things in perspective. But Charlotte really did look as if she'd been through the mill. If only she'd do something with that beautiful blonde hair coiled up on the top of her head. Probably hasn't been to a hairdresser since she was in PTS, poor girl.

'How's the baby?' asked Charlotte.

Jane's face lit up. 'Samantha's fine. Three months old now, and she can lift her head up off the floor and she's trying to crawl . . . I

mustn't go on about her, I'll bore you to tears.'
She looked anxiously at Charlotte, thinking how
much she had to be thankful for, and what a sad
life her friend had experienced.

'I'd love to see her,' Charlotte said eagerly.

'You will; she's asleep in the nursery. I'll bring
her down before you go.' Jane paused, as if
choosing her words carefully. 'You're sure you
want to go over to Cheung Lau today? I mean,
there's no hurry. Stay here for a few days until
you feel rested. You don't have to work at all,
you know. Why not just take a holiday?'

'I want to work as a nurse.' Charlotte's voice
was firm. 'I'm very grateful to you for making
the arrangements at such short notice. One thing
I want to make quite clear, from the start, is
that I don't want any salary. I know that the
Cheung Lau project is a charitable institution,
and I'd like to do something to help.'

'That's very generous of you, but you'll need
something to live on.'

'I've brought enough money for three months.
After that . . .' She shrugged her shoulders
vaguely.

'But a small salary would be useful, I'm sure.
You could buy yourself some new clothes, go
out and enjoy yourself. Do all the things you
wanted to do when you were nursing your
mother.'

Charlotte gave a hoarse laugh. 'No, thanks;
it's not my scene.'

Jane bit her tongue; it wouldn't do to
antagonise her friend at this stage, but she wasn't
going to sit back and watch her becoming more
and more dowdy. She'd been such an attractive,
lively girl when she was eighteen. But she would

have to warn her about Adam. 'There's just a small problem about your appointment at the Cheung Lau hospital,' she began.

Charlotte fixed her round blue eyes on Jane's face expectantly.

'I feel I must warn you that Adam isn't too keen on untrained staff. I think he's had problems with them in the past. He's attached to the World Health Organisation and is used to working in under-developed countries, and he finds it a strain if he's short of trained staff to supervise the 'do-gooders' . . . Jane's voice trailed away in embarrassment. She hadn't meant to use Adam's terminology, but it was too late now.

The hurt showed in Charlotte's eyes. 'Is that what he thinks I am—a "do-gooder"?'

'I'm afraid so; but I was quick to point out that you'd done nearly two years towards your SRN and you'd helped your father in the GP practice . . .'

'It doesn't matter,' Charlotte interrupted wearily. 'As long as he allows me to do some nursing, I shall be quite content.' She found herself dreading the meeting with her boss. He sounded more like a Chinese dragon than an eminent surgeon!

'The baby wake up, madame.' A diminutive Oriental maid stood shyly in the doorway, holding a plump, dimpled baby in her arms.

'Oh, thank you, Wai Yee.' Jane hurried over to take the baby. 'Come to Mummy, there's a good girl.'

The baby gurgled her recognition and gave a wide, toothless smile as she was carried across the room.

'She's lovely!' Charlotte reached out to take Samantha. 'She's got your eyes and Mark's nose!'

Jane laughed. 'Don't start that! Everyone sees someone different in her. Mark's parents over at Shek O are besotted by her. I have to listen to the whole family history when we see them, including the facial distinctions of all of them. Let's go up to the nursery—she needs changing before I feed her.'

The afternoon passed quickly in the pretty pink and white nursery, overlooking Hong Kong harbour. Charlotte watched Jane breast-feeding her delightful daughter and tried not to feel too envious, but it was extremely difficult. She found herself wondering what it must be like to be married to a handsome, successful doctor, to be the mother of his child and live in a fabulous house. She gave a sigh, and Jane looked up from her feeding.

'Is everything all right?' she asked.

Charlotte nodded. 'You look so content like that. It must be wonderful being a mother.'

'It is—you wait till it's your turn!'

Charlotte's eyes filled with tears, and she turned away, but not before Jane had noticed.

'Hey, why so glum? Just be patient. Mr Right will come along one day. Look how long I waited . . . And talking of Mr Right, I can hear Mark down in the hall.' Jane raised her voice. 'We're up here, darling!'

There was the sound of deep male voices on the stairs, and Charlotte barely had time to feel nervous before the two doctors were in the room. She looked across, expecting to see the dragon of her imagination, and her heart started to beat wildly. This was no Chinese dragon! The tall, blond athletic figure looked as if he'd stepped straight off a film set. He crossed the room with long, easy strides and stood towering above her, a cool, enigmatic expression in his deep blue eyes.

'So this is little Nurse Do-good,' he said disparagingly.

Charlotte got to her feet; the effort made the blood drain from her face and she prayed that she wouldn't faint. 'I'm quite tall, actually,' she began, but stopped when she realised what an idiot he must think her. The wretched man hadn't been referring to her stature!

He smiled mockingly as he looked down at her. 'The girl's got spirit, Mark!'

She was aware of her increased heartbeats. He was having a disastrous effect upon her. Would it be possible to work for such a man, in her present circumstances?

Mark seemed uncomfortable at the reaction between them. 'Let me introduce you two; Dr Adam Forster—Nurse Charlotte Craven.'

'My, my, we are being formal!' Dr Forster stretched out his hand and, after a moment's hesitation, Charlotte grasped his fingers. The effect was electrifying; she stared for a second into the depths of his blue eyes before she turned away. It was the strangest experience; almost as if she'd been there before. If she had believed in reincarnation, she would have sworn she'd met this man in a former life. But she didn't believe in it. One life was all you got; one life . . . and when that was over . . .

'I hope you girls have enjoyed your afternoon.' Mark reached down to take his daughter into his arms.

'We've had a good gossip,' Jane smiled lovingly at her husband. 'Would you like some tea?'

'Well, that was the general idea. Let's go out on the balcony.'

'Telephone for Dr Forster, sir.' Chien stood quietly in the doorway.

'Take it in my study, Adam.' Mark handed the baby back to her mother and led the way out of the room.

'What do you think of him?' asked Jane, as soon as the men had disappeared.

Charlotte smiled. 'He's not as bad as I imagined.'

'I'm sorry if we put you off him, but you had to know the worst. Just don't take anything for granted with him. He can be very exacting, or so I'm told. We're very lucky to have him here. I don't know how long we'll be able to keep him, though. He tends to move on once he's got something established, and he's been here for several months already. How long do you plan to stay, by the way?' Jane sounded unconcerned, as she put Samantha back in her cot.

'About three months; then I'll go back. There's a lot to sort out at home, but I needed a complete break, and I wanted to do some nursing before . . .' Charlotte stopped and looked at her friend. Dared she unburden herself? Jane had always been so kind. No, it wasn't fair to worry her. She didn't want anyone to know. 'I'm going to get some fresh air. I'm not used to this air-conditioning.' Charlotte moved out on to the balcony and stared down at the busy city below her. If only people would stop asking questions! she thought. I came away to escape from all that.

'I've got to go back to Cheung Lau.' Dr Forster swept into the room.'

'Oh no! But you haven't had your tea.' Jane was all concern.

'Another time, my dear. Are you ready, Nurse Craven?' He went out on to the balcony and fixed her with a hard, unfriendly stare. 'I'm told I've got to take you with me.'

'Yes, I'm ready.' Charlotte looked up defiantly. He wasn't going to scare her with his pompous attitude; after all, she had nothing to lose. 'I'll get my things.'

Jane watched anxiously, as Charlotte climbed into the car beside Adam Forster. 'Don't forget to come over when you have a day off,' she urged.

'Thanks; I'd love to. See you soon!' Charlotte waved through the window as the car purred away down the drive. She glanced at the stern figure at the wheel. In spite of her initial dislike of the man, she couldn't help admiring his handsome features; the bold thrust of his jaw, the high rugged cheekbones, the commanding presence . . . She turned away. If things had been different, she could have fallen for someone like this. But it was out of the question, now that she had only a year to live.

CHAPTER TWO

THE boat sped across the bay in a haze of fine
blown spray, between the fishing boats and
sampans and out towards the island of Cheung
Lau. Charlotte watched the fascinating coast of
Hong Kong Island disappear as they rounded
the end of Green Island. Quaint old wooden
shacks on stilts clung to the hillside and spilled
down into the sea. Whole families waved as
the boat went past, and she smiled and waved
back. If they can be happy in such primitive
conditions, she thought, so can I.

Dr Forster grinned, and she felt embarrassed
at her childish gesture. 'Do they actually live
in those shacks?' she asked quickly.

'Of course. Hong Kong is grossly over-
populated. They can't all be housed in the new
dwellings, so they make out as best as they
can. Tell me about yourself, Nurse Craven.
Why are you out here?'

His question was so abrupt that it took her
breath away. She could feel her heart pounding.
It was going to be impossible to work for a
man like this! 'My parents died . . .' she began.

'So?' He was still waiting for an answer.

How could he be so callous? 'I needed a
break,' she muttered.

'Why not go on a world cruise? Look for a

rich husband.' His blue eyes held a mocking glint.

'Because I wanted to do some nursing.'

'So why not go and get yourself qualified first? I warn you, I don't make allowances for untrained staff.'

'So I'm told,' she said quietly. 'Don't worry, I've had plenty of experience. I nursed my mother through her final years of mitral stenosis.'

'So, provided all the patients suffer from heart disease, you'll be able to cope, Nurse Craven.' His voice was cool and professional.

'I helped my father run his GP practice, and I did two years of my SRN training . . .'

'Congratulations!' He stood up and went forward to speak to the young Chinese boatman, dismissing her as if she were of no account.

Oh, what's the use? Charlotte thought. She stared out to sea. Why on earth had she come out to this far-flung corner of the world? She could easily have stayed at home and found a nursing job for as long . . . as long as possible. But how long would that be? What had her medical report said? 'The prognosis is poor— perhaps a year . . .' She didn't want to be a burden, as her mother had been. When Julia had taken her nursing finals, maybe she would ask for some help, but until then she was going to be completely independent. She remembered the words scribbled at the bottom of the report. 'The patient should be encouraged to lead a normal life.' That was exactly what she intended to do. No one need know that she had a congenital malformation of the heart. She herself had only found out by chance . . .

'That's Cheung Lau, over there.' Dr Forster had returned and was watching her with a quizzical expression.

She looked out across the water. The sun was slanting low in the sky, spreading a rosy glow over the calm sea and the sails of the fishing vessels making for Cheung Lau harbour. Tiny hills rose out of the bay, shining green and brown in the approaching twilight.

'It looks very picturesque,' she observed.

'You mean, like a picture postcard?'

She nodded warily, knowing that he was going to make fun of her again.

'That's a typical tourist response to the place. We have a great many medical problems to solve, before we can be in any way satisfied.'

The boat nosed its way through the congested harbour, almost scraping the sides of the multi-coloured fishing vessels, their decks awash with children, playing happily in the dying rays of the sun.

Adam Forster leapt off the boat and started to tie the thick mooring rope around a concrete post. Charlotte thought how incongruous his blond good looks were amid the swarthy Oriental fishermen at the quayside. He was wearing cream linen slacks which accentuated the length of his legs. As he straightened his back, he looked like Gulliver in Lilliput, towering above the little people! The young boatman helped her over the side and carried her luggage.

'We have to walk from here; no cars on Cheung Lau,' the doctor said brusquely. 'I'll take the big case. Can you manage this small one?'

'I can walk with you, sir.' The boatman was holding both cases, as if they were as light as a feather.

'That's okay, Jim. You see to the boat. It's not far.'

They walked through the market stalls clustered at the edge of the harbour. Most of them seemed to be selling fish, but here and there they came across a stall crammed with cans of fizzy drinks, shoes, shirts and cigarettes. Beyond the harbour was a grassy clearing, at the foot of a small hill. Bright lights on the perimeter walls shone on to the small white hospital.

'It's not as big as I imagined.' Charlotte paused for a moment, to catch her breath, and put the case down on the beaten earth.

'You should have seen it before it was extended. It started out as a clinic, with only three in-patient beds. Now we've got fifty, and I'm hoping to expand.'

Charlotte noted the pride in Adam Forster's voice. He obviously loved his work. Perhaps she, too, could find some fulfilment here.

'Are you tired?' He sounded almost concerned, as he stared down at her in the gathering dusk.

'A little,' she conceded, bending to pick up the case again.

'Dr Forster!' In the long shadows, Charlotte could see a young man in a white coat running towards them.

'What is it, Nurse Wong?' The doctor hurried to meet him.

'We have taken Mai Ling to the delivery room, sir, and she is asking for you . . .'

'I'm coming. This is Nurse Craven. Show her to her quarters and then take charge of the hospital while I'm in Obstetrics.' He dumped Charlotte's case unceremoniously on the ground and started off up the drive at a rapid pace.

'Can I help?' she asked the departing figure hopefully.

'I doubt it,' was his initial response, but suddenly he paused in front of the main door and turned round. His face held a challenging look as he waited for her to reach him. 'Maybe it would be a good idea to throw you in at the deep end—see what you can do. But if you get in the way . . .'

'I won't. I've helped my father on many occasions.'

'Come with me.' He hurried into the hospital, through the reception area and down a long corridor towards a swing door marked Obstetrics.

'Dr Forster, I'm so glad you made it!' A tall, dark-haired Sister raised her head from examining her patient. 'We're almost ready.'

'Sterile gown, please, and one for Nurse Craven.' He was already scrubbing his hands at the wide sink in the ante-room.

A small Chinese nurse brought sterile gowns and directed Charlotte to another sink, waiting patiently until she had scrubbed up. When she was ready to approach the patient, the doctor was already making his examination. She stopped still, amazed at the sound of his gentle, soothing voice. He was speaking in a strange Oriental language she couldn't understand, and it was having the desired calming effect.

Sister turned to look briefly at Charlotte and

gave her a friendly smile. 'We were having language problems until Dr Forster arrived,' she told her. 'Mai Ling doesn't speak Cantonese or English.'

'That's unusual in Hong Kong, isn't it?'

'Stop chattering and make yourself useful, Nurse Craven.' The doctor's voice changed dramatically. 'Get a bowl and wash Mai Ling's face. The poor girl's covered in sweat.'

'Yes, sir.' Charlotte moved to the head of the delivery table and began to sponge the patient. She smiled comfortingly into the frightened Oriental eyes, hoping to ease some of the tension. What a tiny girl she was! And so young! She couldn't be more than sixteen at the most.

The young girl moaned and clenched her fists tightly, as another contraction began. Charlotte continued to soothe her, while the doctor and the Sister concerned themselves with the delivery. Minutes passed and then, 'We have the head!' Sister sounded pleased with the way things were going, but during the lull in contractions, Mai Ling had started to weep softly to herself.

'There, there—you're going to be all right; not long now.' Charlotte whispered all the helpful phrases she had ever used at a delivery, hoping that in spite of the language barrier, some of her message might get through. She continued to give encouragement as the baby's shoulders and body emerged, wiping away the sweat from the young girl's brow, and then came the moment of triumph.

'It's a girl!' Sister exclaimed happily.

Dr Forster translated this to his patient and

she smiled, all her discomfort forgotten as she reached out thin, bony arms to take her child. She was allowed to cuddle the baby for a few moments before the cord was cut and the tiny nostrils cleansed. The loud healthy wailing was greeted with smiles of pleasure by the attendant medical staff.

Sister picked up an identity label and handed it to Charlotte. 'Fix this on baby's ankle, Nurse.'

'No!' The doctor's voice echoed across the delivery room. 'Mai Ling can't stay here. You should know that, Sister.'

'But I thought . . .'

'I don't care what you thought! I have to take her back. She can stay for a couple of hours.' The harsh voice changed again as he bent over his patient and said something in the strange, sing-song tones. The young mother smiled and nodded as the doctor patted her hand.

Charlotte busied herself with the clearing up, emptying the swabs into a large container in the ante-room. Sister came in to see how she was getting on. 'Making yourself useful, I see. Would you like to help Nurse Lee in the Recovery Room? The patient will not be going back to the ward, apparently.' There was no mistaking the fact that she disagreed with Dr Forster's orders, but was carrying them out, because he was in charge.

Charlotte went through into the recovery room. The pretty Chinese nurse was making up a bed for Mai Ling, and she went across to help fold back the sheet in readiness. They placed a canvas cot at the side of the bed and a side table with a jug of water and a glass.

'I'm going to stay here with Mai Ling,' said Nurse Lee quietly. 'Why don't you go and have some coffee in the staff room? You must be tired after your journey. You'll find it down at the end of the corridor.'

Charlotte flashed her a grateful smile. She was feeling tired, but didn't like to admit it. The staff room was easy to find, and she pushed open the door. Adam Forster was sprawled in an armchair, his long legs reaching out across the polished floor.

'Bring another cup; I've got some coffee here.' He raised himself out of the depths of the armchair and watched her as she came towards him. For the first time he seemed to notice that she was a woman and not just an unqualified nurse who had been wished upon him. 'Help yourself.' He waved his hand towards the jug of steaming coffee.

'Thanks.' Charlotte sank down into a chair, unable to disguise her fatigue. 'That was an interesting delivery.'

'In what way?' The deep blue eyes fixed themselves on her face.

She had merely meant to start a polite conversation, but the look he was giving her put her on her guard. 'Well, for a start, the patient was extremely young . . .'

'Almost sixteen,' he barked defensively.

'Still quite young, by European standards.'

'But we're not in Europe. This is Asia, or hadn't you noticed? Life is not quite so cosy out here. There's real suffering, intense poverty . . .' He broke off, aware that his impassioned tone was alarming her. 'You wouldn't understand,' he muttered.

'Not unless you explain it to me—and I'm willing to learn.'

He smiled, a long languid expression that made the tough features almost boyish. 'I can see that. I liked the way you helped out in the delivery room. Maybe you'll be of some use to us, after all.'

'I intend to be,' she replied firmly. 'Tell me, why can't Mai Ling stay here in the hospital?'

'That's none of your business, and I'd be grateful if you forget that she ever came here.' His tone was curt and dismissive. 'Leave the running of the hospital to me. Concentrate on your nursing, and don't poke your nose into things that don't concern you.'

An ominous silence descended on the room. Charlotte was seething with indignation. How was she going to find out anything if she didn't ask questions? And how was she to know where to draw the line between administrative matters and medical theory? What an aggravating man! She got up quietly and walked over to the window. A pale moon shone down from a cloudless sky, as she went out on to the verandah. She could hear the gentle lapping of the waves on the nearby shore.

It's so peaceful, she thought, with a pang of sadness. Maybe my senses are sharper now that I know I haven't got long to live. If only I could wake up and find I'd dreamt it all! But no, I saw the medical report with my own eyes. She remembered that fateful morning when she had opened the morning mail in the surgery. Her father's partner had arranged for her to have a set of tests to determine why she was feeling so run down after the death of her parents. She had read her name at the top of the page, and then the scribbled notes that were to change her life.

'All the signs point to a congenital heart malformation. Surgery is inadvisable at the present time . . .'

'You're looking very thoughtful.' Adam Forster was standing behind her in the moonlight, his face softened by an expression of tenderness. He had been watching her for some time, wondering what it was that was eating away at her. Perhaps she'd had an unfortunate love affair. 'What are you worrying about?'

He was standing very close, too close for comfort. Charlotte looked up into his eyes and her pulses raced. She couldn't tell him that she was worrying about the fact that she had torn up the report as soon as she had read it, determined that no one else should know; determined that no one should send for her sister to come home from hospital to look after her, as she had been when her mother was ill. But supposing she had been wrong? Supposing she hadn't read it correctly? No, there was no doubt about it. Her name, Charlotte Craven, had been there in bold type at the top of the page. She hadn't dreamed it; it was a living nightmare. A tear sprang unbidden to her eye and she turned her head.

'I don't mean to pry, but I always take an interest in the welfare of my staff.' Adam Forster's voice had taken on his professional tone, but there was a genuine concern in his manner, as he reached forward to wipe away the revealing tear with a large white, masculine handkerchief.

She flinched at the unexpected gesture and he smiled down at her. 'If there's anything I can do . . .'

'There isn't,' she said firmly. 'I'm just tired, that's all. I think I'll go to my room. It's been a long day.'

'Of course.' He was standing so close that she could almost hear the beating of his heart. A strange shiver ran down her spine. It was so romantic to be standing here in the moonlight with this tall, disturbing man. Was this what sexual attraction felt like? She didn't know; there had never been time to find out, during the long years of her domestic incarceration. Whatever it was, it was deliciously sensual to feel the unusual warmth spreading through her entire body . . .

'Let me show you the way.' He was walking over to the door and reluctantly she followed. For a fraction of a second she had hoped he might kiss her out there under the pale moon . . .

She gave a little secret smile to herself. I'm becoming so stupid! she scolded herself. It must be because I'm about as experienced as a retarded teenager!

'What's so funny?' He turned at the door, to stare down at her, wondering at the sudden change of mood.

'Nothing,' she said lightly. 'Which way?'

She followed him down the corridor and out on to a verandah which ran the length of the hospital. The staff quarters were at the end. Charlotte caught a glimpse of some of the hospital rooms and a small operating theatre as they hurried past, and then Adam Forster stopped in front of some french windows whose bright gingham curtains looked strangely out of place in the sterile hospital atmosphere.

'Your room. Nurse Lee sleeps next door, so if there's anything you need . . .' He stood back so that she could walk inside. 'You're on duty at eight tomorrow. Don't be late.' On impulse, he reached down and brushed his lips across her cheek. The poor girl looked so lost and lonely. Perhaps he'd been too hard on her, he was thinking, as he hurried away, hoping she wouldn't misinterpret his friendly gesture. He couldn't allow personal feelings to obscure his professionalism.

Charlotte watched as he disappeared round the corner of the hospital building, before she raised a hand and touched the place where his lips had been. Had he really meant to kiss her? Her heart was beating madly. What a disturbing effect he had on her! She wondered how long she could survive, literally, working with such a man, as she stepped into the little room. A small bamboo chair occupied the centre of the room; a narrow bed was pushed against one wall, while on the other side was a simple cane table which served as a dressing table. It was a cool, unsophisticated room, but there was a welcoming feeling as she surveyed its simplicity. She climbed between the cotton sheets and lay staring up at the white ceiling, listening to the unfamiliar sounds of the night.

From somewhere on the hillside she could hear a dog howling, and then came another animal noise, nearer to the hospital. Yes, it was quite definitely horses' hooves pounding on the beaten earth. How strange, at this time of night! And then she remembered Adam Forster's words: 'I have to take her back.' Back where? she wondered, as she heard the quiet voice of the doctor out there, beyond the window.

There was the tiny, shrill cry of a baby. Charlotte was wide awake now, as she pushed open her window. In the moonlight she could just make out the outline of a horse and cart moving off down the hospital drive. Don't poke your nose into things that don't concern you, he had said.

She sighed and went back to bed, but it was a long time before she was able to sleep.

CHAPTER THREE

THE sun was streaming in through the gingham curtains when Charlotte awoke. My God! she thought. What time is it? She reached for her watch. Seven o' clock—thank heavens for that! Adam Forster had told her not to be late, and she wanted to make a good impression on her first day. She rolled over on her back and lay gazing at the whitewashed ceiling. A large black fly was buzzing around the central light bulb. The air was already warm. It felt like the middle of the day. She remembered yesterday; her arrival in Hong Kong, the meeting with Dr Forster. Every detail of his handsome face was etched firmly in her mind. She had never known anyone to have such a striking effect on her before. Hardly surprising, she thought, smiling inwardly. I haven't been anywhere to meet anyone for so long.

She stretched her long legs languidly in the bed. When she had first been at St. Catherine's she had met a few students and doctors who had interested her. She'd been out on many occasions—even in PTS—but always in groups or a foursome. There had never been anyone who had stirred any romantic feelings within her. She jumped out of bed and padded along the corridor in her bare feet to take a shower.

Pull yourself together, girl! she told herself. You must be suffering from jet-lag.

Sister Benson was sitting at the long table in the staff dining room. She smiled a welcome when she saw Charlotte.

'Good morning, Nurse Craven. Did you sleep well?'

'Yes, thank you, Sister. I went out like a light.'

'You must have been exhausted. It was just like Dr Forster to throw you in at the deep end like that.'

'I expect he wanted to see what I was made of,' said Charlotte. 'It was nice to feel useful again.'

'Again?' Sister Benson looked enquiringly at her new nurse.

'I've rather been kicking my heels since . . .' she paused uncertainly, and took a deep breath, before continuing, 'since my parents died. It's great to be back in harness.'

'I'm glad you think so. Coffee?'

Charlotte nodded, and held out her cup. They were the only staff in the dining room, she noticed. 'What time do the others have breakfast?' she asked.

Sister laughed. 'Some of them don't. They prefer to lie in till the very last minute.'

'I would have thought Dr Forster would be here.' Charlotte tried to sound only casually interested.

'He's not back yet,' Sister replied abruptly.

Not back. Charlotte frowned. Back from where? Where was it he went last night? She buttered a piece of toast, not daring to ask.

'I expect you'd like to look round the hospital

before you start work.' Sister's calm voice interrupted her speculations. 'I shall be busy in Outpatients all morning, but I'll ask Nurse Lee to take you round, as soon as she puts in an appearance. Ah, talk of the devil . . .'

The pretty young Chinese nurse came through the doorway and sat down beside Charlotte. She was wearing the same white cotton uniform dress, but round her slim waist there was a navy blue webbing belt, clasped with a silver buckle, to denote that she was a trained nurse. The silver badge of State Registration was pinned to her lapel, alongside the purple badge of her London training school. All of a sudden Charlotte began to feel insecure. She had no paper qualifications at all, not unless you counted prelim exams, and it was years since she'd passed those. 'I was just telling Nurse Craven that you would take her round the hospital this morning.'

'Of course, Sister. I'd be delighted.' The Oriental eyes swept over the new nurse. She looks very shy and unsure of herself, and she's so far from home. Rather like I was when I first went over to England, Suzie Lee was thinking. I'll try and make her feel at home.

Male Nurse Chien Wong poked his head round the door. 'Sergeant Leung is here, Sister. He wants to know . . .'

The khaki-clad figure of the island policeman strode unceremoniously into the room. Sister Benson got to her feet, her eyes glinting with annoyance at the intrusion.

'No need to get up, Sister. I thought I might find you here. May I?' He indicated his wish to join them at the table.

Helen Benson recovered her composure. 'Of course. Would you like some coffee, sergeant?'

'No, no, I mustn't stay long. I have work to do.' His eyes searched the room. 'I really wanted to speak with Dr Forster.'

'I'm afraid he's not available at the moment. Can I help you?' Sister asked calmly.

'I am preparing my census of the island population,' he began importantly. 'I would like to see your records of admissions and discharges during the last year.'

'And what is the purpose of this census?' Helen Benson was unable to conceal her disapproval.

The policeman smiled politely. 'That I cannot reveal, at this stage. One cannot be too careful.'

'I will ask the doctor to produce the record book for your inspection—and now, if you will excuse me, I have to brief my staff.' Sister moved to the door and stood waiting, expectantly.

'Of course.' He paused in the doorway beside her. 'Ah, just one little detail, Sister; did you admit anyone yesterday?'

'No admissions yesterday.' She turned her back on the policeman and started to walk off down the corridor. 'My report starts in two minutes, nurses.'

The khaki figure hovered for an instant before jamming his peaked cap on his head and following in her wake.

'We'd best get a move on.' Suzie Lee gulped down her coffee. 'Sister's very good-tempered, except when she gets caught up in red tape.'

Charlotte smiled. 'You mean like now?'

'Exactly.'

Sister was waiting for them in the reception

area. 'Of all the nerve!' She was positively trembling with anger. 'How dare he walk into *my* hospital like that!'

Charlotte glanced at the retreating figure on the hospital drive, wondering if Sister had managed to conceal her irritation from him.

'The hospital is divided into areas dealing with medical, surgical and obstetrics—as you might expect—but because we have only fifty beds, we have to be fairly fluid in our interpretation of the divisions.'

The report was mainly for the benefit of the new nurse, and Helen Benson warmed to her subject, forgetting her annoyance and concentrating all her teaching skill. The girl looked as if she wanted to be a good nurse. Certainly, from what she had seen of her performance last night, she showed promise. She explained how the hospital had been the brainchild of Dr Frobisher's father, who had funded the initial construction and set up a charitable trust. They were expanding all the time, as the need arose.

'. . . And so, if you'd like to do a quick tour of the building, you could then help out in the medical section, which is usually our busiest. As I said, most of the difficult surgical work goes to our sister hospital, St Margaret's on the Peak, on Hong Kong, but most of our medical cases prefer to stay here, close to their relatives. Obstetrics is usually full, but they don't stay long and they're up and about before we've time to put the baby in a cot. These Chinese women could teach the girls back home a thing or two!'

'How is Mai Ling?' Charlotte had listened to the report, hopeful that she would learn

something of the young mother's condition. The
reference to the obstetrics department had
renewed her interest.

Sister Benson's eyes took on a veiled look.
'Who?' she asked severely.

Charlotte dared not reply. Don't poke your
nose in, said the warning voice inside her. Dr
Forster told you to mind your own business.

'Let's start our round.' Nurse Lee jumped
briskly to her feet, saving the situation. 'This
way, Nurse Craven.'

Charlotte followed the tiny figure thankfully.
They went along the main corridor, calling in to
see various interesting cases in surgery, briefly
visiting the small theatre, spending far too long
in Obstetrics and ending up in Medical.

'I'll leave you here with Sister Chen. She'll
take care of you.'

'Thanks very much.' Charlotte watched her
new-found friend disappearing through the swing
doors, feeling suddenly very lost.

Sister Chen smiled at the new nurse. She had
been told to expect an unqualified volunteer,
and to supervise her as much as possible; only to
give her the simplest of tasks, and to report any
misdemeanours to Dr Forster himself. The girl
looked older than she had imagined. Not married,
so she'd been told. Strange she hadn't found
time to get herself qualified. Must have done
something else. Sister Chen gave a sigh of
resignation. What on earth was she supposed to
do with her?

'Have you ever given a blanket bath, Nurse?'
she asked.

What a strange question! 'Of course, Sister.'

Charlotte looked puzzled. What does she take take me for? she thought. A complete idiot?

'Good. Then perhaps you would help Nurse Chu with Mr Jiang in bed three.' Sister Chen turned dismissively.

'What's his diagnosis?' asked Charlotte.

Sister Chen's eyes narrowed. It was the first time she had been asked such a question before a simple bed-bath. She stared at the new recruit, hoping that she wasn't going to have to waste too much time on her. On the other hand, she might be genuinely interested in nursing as a career, in which case, she would help her all she could.

'Mr Jiang suffered a cardiac arrest six days ago. His oxygen has been discontinued, but he is on complete bed rest. If you would care to read up on his medication, the notes are in my office.'

'Thank you, Sister.'

'*After* the blanket bath, that is.'

'Of course.' Charlotte hurried over to bed three. Why did she have to come up against this wall of mistrust? She was only trying to be helpful, and she couldn't help having an enquiring mind. She wanted to know all she could about her patients; that was the only way to be of any use to them.

Nurse Chu had assembled the trolley and laundry basket by the patient's bedside. She looked up and smiled, pleased that she was going to get some help. Mr Jiang was very thin, but even so it would be difficult to cope on her own.

'I'm Nurse Craven,' she told her.

'I know,' the young nurse grinned. The whole hospital had been told to expect this latest in the long list of volunteers. It was to be hoped that this one wouldn't be frightened away by Dr Forster's caustic comments. 'Take hold of this sheet, will you, and roll him over towards me.'

Charlotte smiled encouragingly at the patient, who was looking decidedly alarmed. 'Do you speak English?' she asked hopefully.

Mr Jiang's thin blue lips made some response to the obvious question, but his reply was unintelligible. Nurse Chu spoke to him in Cantonese, and he nodded.

'I've just explained what's happening,' she told Charlotte. 'I think he thought he was in for a major operation.'

'I hope you'll give as much care to the procedure as you would to a major operation.'

Dr Forster's voice behind them took them both by surprise. Charlotte looked up into the deep blue eyes and her pulses began to race.

'I'm glad to see you being of some use to us. I suppose you've done a blanket bath before?'

'Many times, sir.'

'Splendid!'

She couldn't decide whether he was being sarcastic or not, as she turned her attention away. He looked tired; there was a thick blond stubble on his chin—obviously he hadn't had time to shave yet. He must have come straight into hospital from his mysterious assignment. His white coat was open at the front, revealing a crumpled cotton shirt. Charlotte reached for the soap and started to lather a cloth, aware that he was watching her and wishing he would move away. Heaven knew how she would feel if she were doing something really difficult!

'I'd like to see the patients for discharge today,

Sister,' he said. 'We're going to be short of beds
if we don't get a move on . . .'

Thank goodness, he was moving away. Charlotte breathed a sigh of relief as she bent over
her patient. Mr Jiang was pathetically thin. She
wondered if there was anyone at home to look
after him. It was so difficult when you couldn't
converse with the patient, but the grateful look
in his eyes as they made him comfortable against
clean pillowcases spoke wonders. She handed
him a glass of water.

'Got to keep drinking, Mr Jiang.' He smiled,
and put the glass to his lips. She marked the
fluid content down on the intake and output
chart. It wasn't so very different from UK
nursing after all, she thought, as they moved on
to the next patient.

She trundled the trolley into the sluice when
the bed-baths were finished. Dr Forster was still
with Sister discussing a difficult case.

'Come and have some coffee,' Charlotte heard
Sister say, but he was shaking his head.

'Haven't had breakfast yet. I'll be along later.'

She watched through the window in the sluice
door as the tall, athletic figure disappeared.

'He's very good-looking, don't you think?'
Nurse Chu gave her a knowing smile.

'I suppose so; hadn't really thought about it.
What's next on the agenda?' she asked briskly,
dumping the dirty linen in the huge square
basket.

'I'll show you how to take TPRs and then you
can help me with them.'

'I can take TPRs.' Charlotte's voice was quietly
patient. Ye gods, was there no end to the

humiliation? She'd been taking TPRs while this little nurse was still at school!

'I'd better check with Sister to see if it's all right for you to do them.' Nurse Chu looked doubtful as she hurried away.

Charlotte finished tidying up the sluice and emerged in time to hear Sister say, 'You'd better stay with her. Dr Forster said she was to be supervised . . . Ah, there you are, Nurse Craven. The patients have their own thermometers, of course, and we take the temperature under the tongue . . .'

Sister's voice droned on. I shouldn't be ungrateful, Charlotte thought. She's only trying to help. When they find out how experienced I am, they'll give me more responsibility, perhaps.

She got through the TPR round, glad of the chance to get to know some of the patients. To her relief, she found that language was not too big a problem. Some of the patients spoke English and were anxious to talk to her.

'You come from England?' asked a small, round-faced lady, beaming in a friendly way at the new nurse. She's very pretty, she was thinking as she watched her shaking down the thermometer. 'Do you have husband?'

Charlotte smiled. 'No, Mrs Wu.' She glanced down at the notes: Wu Wai Yee, aged 65, rheumatoid arthritis. Strange how the Chinese put the surname before the given names. She looked back at the dimpled face and contented Oriental eyes. 'Do *you* have a husband?' she asked. It seemed a good topic of conversation.

'Of course! And many children.' Mrs Wu launched into a long description of her sons, their wives, her grandchildren, her beautiful daughters . . .

'Nurse Craven, when you can tear yourself away, I'd like you to tidy the linen cupboard.'

Charlotte was startled by the severity of Sister's voice. Surely it wasn't a crime to take an interest in her patients. She patted Mrs Wu's hand, in a gesture of resignation, before hurrying after the blue-clad figure.

'There is no time to waste in this hospital. Please remember that.' Sister Chen pushed open the linen cupboard door. 'Deal with one shelf at a time. Remove all the linen; shake it, fold it and put it back neatly.'

'Yes, Sister.' Charlotte looked at the sheets and pillowcases on the top shelf. They appeared to be immaculate. What on earth was the point of the exercise, unless it were to keep her fully occupied away from the patients? She tried to drum up some enthusiasm for the task, but it wasn't easy. By lunchtime she was ready to scream with frustration.

'You can take your off duty this afternoon, Nurse Craven, and come back this evening at five.' Sister stared critically round the linen shelves. 'Hm, not bad.' She reached over and straightened the corner of a sheet, which was slightly out of line, before she turned away dismissively.

Charlotte went quickly to her little room. She felt hot and tired, but not hungry, and she had no intention of going to the dining room for lunch. What she needed most of all was a swim in the sea. Yes, a cool dip in the cleansing ocean would restore her spirits more than food. And she could find a snack of some kind on the beach, probably.

She tossed her white cotton uniform on the bed and pulled off the restricting cap. Her hair tumbled down from its pins in a golden cascade as she reached for a ribbon to tie it back.

There was no one at the front of the hospital to see her run down the drive in her casual shorts and top, for which she was grateful. There was barely room in her shoulder-bag for a bikini and a small hand towel, but she had stuffed them in anyway, and managed to close the zip. She was feeling better already, as she followed the little path though the clearing. There must be a quiet beach on the other side of this little hill, she was thinking, as she strode forward with long, swinging strides, revelling in the feeling of freedom. I don't want to go to the crowded beach by the town, she thought. Too many tourists.

She reached the top of the grassy knoll in a matter of minutes and gazed down at the blue sea lapping up on a deserted beach. Just what the doctor ordered! she smiled. Funny, I haven't thought about my health all morning. That's a good sign! She ran down the little path between the dry grass and flung herself down on the warm sand. Way out to sea there was a fishing boat with red and orange sails, but otherwise she was completely alone. She stripped off and plunged into the sea.

Oh, this was wonderful! She swam out with steady strokes, glorying in the soothing, salty water as it rippled over her. The sky looked deliciously blue as she turned on her back and lay motionless watching a stray white cloud as it drifted across from the Peak. Her eyes closed; suddenly she felt sleepy, and decided to stretch out on the sand.

She must have been asleep for about an hour when the sound of voices awakened her. Raising herself on her elbow, she stared at a group of children by the water. They were chattering to each other in high-pitched, excited voices and they hadn't seen Charlotte in the shade of a huge rock. She shook the sand from her body as she stood up and made her way back to the sea. Perhaps they could tell her where she could buy some food. She was decidedly peckish now.

'*Wei*!' she began uncertainly, remembering from her phrase book the Cantonese for 'hello'.

The chattering stopped immediately, and the children regarded her with a mixture of horror and suspicion, as if she was a creature from outer space.

She moved towards them and stretched out a hand. '*Bin gor sik gong ying mun* ?' Would they understand, in spite of her atrocious accent, that she wanted to know if anyone spoke English?

The tallest boy took charge of the situation by grabbing a small child in each hand and chasing off along the shoreline. The others followed, calling to each other as they ran. When they reached the end of the small cove, they scrambled up the hillside and disappeared among the bushes.

How strange! Charlotte watched them until they were all out of sight. So what was all that about? Had she got two heads or something? She'd never had that effect on children before. Perhaps it was her Cantonese! She grinned to herself and determined to do something about it. If she spent a few minutes a day with the cassettes she'd brought with her and the grammer book . . .

'What's so funny?' The tall, athletic figure in front of her seemed to have materialised from nowhere.

'Why, Dr Forster, I didn't expect to see you here.' She smoothed a hand over her long hair, aware of the masculine glint in his eyes as they swept over her bikini.

'You seemed amused by something, when I came down the path just now.' He leaned languidly against the rock, looking more like a carefree playboy in his hip-hugging shorts than an eminent surgeon.

'There were the strangest children here a moment ago,' she told him. 'When I spoke to them, they were terrified. I felt so sorry for them, I mean I didn't mean them any harm.' She was speaking in a quick jerky voice, intensely aware of the scrutiny of his deep blue eyes.

He took a step forward and smiled down at her. 'I think you must have been dreaming. There are no children on this side of the island. It's quite deserted, as you can see. Have you been swimming?'

'Yes, but . . .' Charlotte wanted to pursue the episode of the children. It hadn't been a dream. True, she'd been to sleep, but she had been wide awake when she saw them, there by the water.

Adam Forster was peeling off his shorts to reveal tight black swimming trunks. 'Come and cool off in the water,' he invited.

She hesitated for a moment, as she watched the lithe figure sprinting towards the sea. Every taut muscle was rippling as he plunged in and swam, vigorously away from the shore. Dismissing her problem with a shake of her long blonde hair, she raced after him. The sea was warm in the afternoon rays of the sun, as she swam parallel to the beach, not wanting to go out to where the doctor was now resting on his back. When she heard his sweeping strokes through the water, she turned her head.

'I didn't know you were an outdoor enthusiast.' The fair head above the surface of the sea was dangerously close to hers.

Charlotte trod water. 'I enjoy the sea and the fresh air, when I've been cooped up all morning.'

'How did you get on with Sister Chen?'

Was it possible that she was having this relaxed conversation with the great man? Maybe he changed his personality in the water, or perhaps when he shed his clothes. Certainly he was very human, at the moment. Almost too human for her liking! She saw the warmth in his eyes as he took another stroke towards her. He was only a man, after all, and an intensely desirable one at that! And she had, after all, had no experience with men. Did he really care how she'd got on with the exacting Sister, or was he just making conversation?

'I . . . er . . . I found her demanding . . . but very fair,' she added hastily.

He laughed easily. 'A fair assessment, I would say. Race you back to the shore!'

She saw his tousled hair on the surface of the water, as he streaked away from her. Inevitably he was way ahead of her as she ran, laughing up the beach.

He turned and caught hold of her hands. 'You

look so much younger when you laugh. Almost
like a young girl. Why are you out here,
Charlotte?'

She took a deep breath when she heard him
using her name. It seemed strange on his lips.
But then he seemed strange this afternoon; quite
different from the dragon of a doctor she had
imagined him to be. But, like everyone else, he
asked too many questions. Charlotte pulled away
her hands and ran them irritably through her
long hair. He didn't answer her questions. Why
should she answer his? He might be her boss at
the hospital, but here, on this deserted beach,
she was her own boss. Let him think what he
liked!

'It's a secret,' she said playfully.

He smiled knowingly and pulled her down
beside him on the sand. 'You were crossed in
love.' His voice was insincere and dramatic.
They both knew they were play-acting.

'I don't know how I can bear it!' She gave a
little giggle, and, amazingly, he entered into the
spirit of the thing.

'Hong Kong is the place to recover from a
broken love affair,' he teased.

'That's what I thought.' She smiled brazenly
up into his blue eyes, rejoicing in the tenderness
she saw there. Oh, this is fun! I'm so enjoying
myself, she thought. She gave a little wriggle of
pleasure in the sand and he leaned across her.

'You remind me of my mother.'

'Thanks very much!' she rejoined, sarcastically.

'I meant it as a compliment. She was a very
beautiful woman.' His tone was soft and gentle.
He picked up a handful of sand and let it run
abstractedly through his fingers.

'Was?' she queried, watching the fine sand as it slipped back on to the beach.

A faraway look came into his eyes. 'She died when I was very young, but I remember her long fair hair. My grandmother took care of me. She was Swedish—that's where the blonde hair comes from. Is this your natural colour?' He took a few strands of her hair in his fingers and examined it earnestly, as it it were a biopsy under the microscope.

'Of course,' Charlotte replied quickly. He didn't think she was blonde from a bottle, surely!

'You're not the artificial type, are you?' He smiled into her eyes, then seemed to remember who she was: the difficult do-gooder he hadn't wanted in the first place. But she was more intelligent than he'd expected. He'd like to find more about her backround. 'Your father was a GP, I gather?'

'Yes.' He's fishing again, she thought warily.

'Any brothers or sisters?'

'One sister—she takes her finals at St Catherine's Hospital this year. She's twenty-one.'

'That must be quite a blow, having a little sister who's better qualified than you are.'

'Not really. I'm happy for her,' Charlotte replied dutifully. Did he know he'd hit the nail on the head? She turned away, so that he couldn't see her sad expression.

The sun was beginning to slant down over the sea, casting a rosy glow on the shore. 'It's time we were getting back.' Adam Forster stood up determinedly, unwilling to prolong this dangerous encounter. The girl was getting through to him. Dammit, he didn't want any more complications! His life was complicated enough as it was, without getting involved in a useless romance. He pulled on his shorts and set off up the path. 'Keep close behind me. There may be some snakes, but if we make a noise they'll go away. They're more frightened of us than we are of them.'

Charlotte dragged on her shorts and top, hastily, and hurried up the path. Adam Forster paused halfway up to wait for her, a strange, enigmatic smile on his lips. Her heart beat rapidly. Wouldn't it be terrible if I collapsed here on the hillside? she thought, as she caught up with him. He would have to resuscitate me, give me cardiac massage, mouth-to-mouth breathing and then carry me in his arms back to hospital. She shivered involuntarily.

'Are you cold?' He sounded concerned.

She shook her head. 'On the contrary.' The dying sun was on the back of her head as she followed him over the hill and back to civilisation. She felt hungry, and realised that she hadn't had any lunch. Too late now! It was almost five o' clock. Sister Chen would be on the warpath if she were late.

He went round the back of the hospital to his quarters, without saying goodbye. Probably doesn't want to be seen with me, she thought miserably. Oh well, back to the grind!

Sister was waiting for her when she arrived back on Medical. It had been a rush to shower away the salt from her skin and get into uniform.

'Your cap's crooked, Nurse.'

'I'm sorry. I hadn't much time . . .'

'You've had all afternoon. I hope you're feeling refreshed, because we're busy this evening. Help Nurse Chu with the beds and backs and then report to me when you've finished.' Sister reached forward and tugged Charlotte's cap into position as if she were a recalcitrant child. 'There, that's better!'

'Thank you, Sister.' She went across to join up with Nurse Chu.

'Did you have a nice afternoon?' the young nurse asked, in a friendly manner.

Charlotte smiled. 'Mm. I went for a walk—and a swim.'

'How energetic! I went to sleep. I like to take a siesta when I'm off duty; recharge the batteries.'

'That's what I should have done.' But no. It had been an interesting experience. She remembered Adam Forster's lithe, muscular body as he plunged into the sea.

'How are you this evening, Mrs Wu?' She forced her attention back to the patient.

'I'm very uncomfortable.' The high-pitched voice had a whining tone.

'Did you sit out in a chair this afternoon?'

'Yes, but it's not the same as going for a walk. I feel so stiff!' Mrs Wu grimaced the rotund features and clenched her distorted fingers.

'We'll soon put you right,' said Charlotte, breezily. 'Take hold of my arm and roll towards me . . . that's right. Nurse Chu is going to rub your back.'

'Let's have a look at those pressure points.' Sister hurried over from her desk. 'Hm . . . Cod liver oil, I think . . .'

'Oh, don't you have any . . .' Charlotte stopped herself, just in time. The angry look on Sister's face warned her she was way out of line. But—cod liver oil on a bedsore! It was archaic! There

were far more effective and pleasanter ways of
dealing with the problem.

'You were saying, Nurse?'

She took a deep breath. 'I've always found
cod liver oil to be . . . er . . . rather unpleasant.
I mean, the smell, for a start, whereas if we
were to use . . .'

'In my training school we always used it.' The
Oriental eyes narrowed to mere slits. 'The old
remedies are often the best, as you'll find when—
or if—you ever take the time to get yourself
properly trained.' And Sister swept away, shaking
with indignation at the audacity of the girl.

Nurse Chu picked up the bottle of cod liver
oil and looked across the patient at Charlotte
with a sympathetic grin. As she bent to apply
the liquid, she whispered, 'She's an old battleaxe,
and she's gunning for you, so watch your step.'

Charlotte pursed her lips. She would have to
think before she spoke in future. She looked
down at Mrs Wu. Poor woman! It must be awful
to be crippled with rheumatoid arthritis, unable
to get out and about. She took extra care making
her comfortable when the pressure points had
been dealt with, plumping up the pillows and
settling her back in a clean nightdress.

'How long you been nurse?' asked Mrs Wu,
when the procedure was almost finished.

'Oh . . . let me see, on and off for nine years.
I started training when I was eighteen, but I had
to go home after a couple of years to nurse my
mother and help my father—he was a doctor.'

'I think you very good nurse.' The patient
was smiling happily, now that she felt more
comfortable.

'Thank you.' Oh lord, Sister's looking across

again! thought Charlotte. I must be chatting too much. She smiled a hasty farewell and pushed the trolley on to the next patient.

The evening flew quickly in a flurry of beds and backs, suppers and settling the patients down. Almost time to go off duty. Charlotte glanced at the clock on the wall.

'I'd like you to clean the sluice, Nurse Craven.'

'Yes, Sister.' Her response was automatic. If she'd been asked to perform a major operation she would have complied, at this moment in time! But oh, she was so hungry! Only another few minutes. What did she mean by 'clean'?

She surveyed the chaos by the sink. Test tubes for urine-testing lurked amid cotton wool swabs and bottles of carbolic. Oh well, here goes! she thought. She tidied everything away, washing the test tubes, and discarding the rubbish. When she had finished, she stood back to admire her handiwork. That was better! All neat and tidy now.

'What about the floor?'

She jumped as she heard Sister's voice behind her. 'The floor, Sister?'

'The surface upon which you are standing.'

Charlotte stared down at the blue and white tiles. There was no litter on it; she'd picked up a couple of errant swabs. It looked all right to her.

'I'd like you to wash the floor.'

'But I thought . . .' She bit her tongue. I thought that was the cleaner's job, she had been going to say. Never in her life had she been asked to wash a floor in hospital. Perhaps it was standard procedure out here.

'You'll find a mop and bucket in that

cupboard.' The door of the sluice swung closed again.

Charlotte stuck the bucket under the tap, fuming inwardly. This wasn't how she'd imagined her life in Hong Kong! She squeezed out the mop and swung it viciously across the floor. Backwards and forwards . . . oh, she felt so tired!

The door opened again. 'Mind the floor; it's wet.' She stopped in mid-swipe, gazing in embarrassment at the tall, white-coated doctor.

'What do you think you're doing?' His voice was stern.

She stared at the piercing blue eyes. Was this the man who had raced her to the beach after their idyllic swim? She barely recognised the smoothed-back fair hair from the tousled locks, covered in sand. 'I'm . . . I'm cleaning the floor.' What did he think she was doing, for heaven's sake!

'Don't you know we have cleaners to perform such menial tasks in this hospital?' His voice was ominously calm.

'Well, I thought you might have, but . . .' Oh, heavens! She didn't want to upset Sister again.

'What's the trouble?' Sister's dark head appeared round the door. 'Ah, Dr Forster, I never saw you come in.' Her manner changed completely as she smiled ingratiatingly at her favourite doctor.

'How long have you been allowing your nurses to wash the floor, Sister?'

Allowing your nurses! Charlotte suppressed a smile. He made it sound like an honour! She leaned on the mop, enjoying Sister's discomfiture.

'I had to give the girl something to do.

Without supervision she can't do anything difficult, and we're very short-staffed, as you know . . .'

'There's no need for a nurse to wash the floor. Her time can be put to better use than that, Sister Chen. I think you will find Nurse Craven is more experienced than you expected.'

Sister drew in a sharp breath, but did not reply. Oh, the ignominy of it! she was thinking. *He* was the one who'd told her to supervise the new recruit, and give her simple tasks. Well, you couldn't find anything simpler than washing the sluice floor. And now, while her back was turned—well, she'd only gone down the corridor for a couple of minutes to have a quick coffee with Sister Benson, and along he comes, poking his nose into the running of her ward. If you ask me, he's taken a fancy to her, with her long blonde hair, falling out of her cap. Ridiculous, having hair that long at her age! I can see I'm going to have trouble with this one! She found her voice at last.

'It's time you went off duty, Nurse.'

'I'll just finish this . . .' Charlotte began, but strong arms wrenched the mop from her hands.

'Go off duty, Nurse Craven.' Adam Forster was accustomed to instant obedience.

'Would you like to go round the patients, Doctor?' Sister asked quickly.

'I've completed my round already; I couldn't find you. Is there anything you wish to discuss?'

'Not at the moment.'

'Then I'll say goodnight.'

Sister watched him following the new nurse down the corridor and shook her head. Doctors! She'd never understand them. You try to carry out their orders to the letter, and then they turn round and humiliate you. Maybe she could get Nurse Craven moved . . .

Charlotte quickened her step. Food, that was all she wanted!

'Nurse Craven!'

She turned at the sound of his voice.

'What's the rush?' He stared down at her, an amused smile playing on his lips.

'I'm starving! I didn't have any lunch.' She slipped easily into a relaxed rapport with the eminent doctor, now that they were off the ward.

'That wasn't very wise,' he observed.

'No, it wasn't. I'd better get a move on before they finish supper.'

'I've got a better idea. Go and change out of your uniform and I'll take you out for supper.' Even as Adam spoke, he was beginning to regret it. What had got into him today? This was the girl's first day in hospital. Supposing she got the wrong idea . . .

'That would be lovely. Where shall I see you?' Her heart was turning somersaults! She tried not to look too excited.

'Come to my room when you're ready.' His voice was brisk. He'd have to go through with it now.

CHAPTER FOUR

WHATEVER should she wear? Charlotte gazed in desperation at her inadequate wardrobe. It was so long since she had been out to supper with anyone other than her father's friends. Where would Adam take her? She couldn't imagine he intended going over to Hong Kong Island, but you never knew. Perhaps the tweed skirt with her silk blouse? It was what her mother called a good classic outfit, but she'd had it quite a few years. She'd have to take Jane up on her offer of a shopping outing; find out what people were wearing nowadays. In the end, she compromised, and wore the silk blouse with her cream linen skirt. It had been new last summer, so it was possibly still in fashion. She let down her long hair and brushed it viciously, to make it shine.

Can't think why I'm in such a tizzy, she was thinking. I'm only going out for a bite to eat. Her appetite seemed to have evaporated all of a sudden, to be replaced by a feeling of nervous excitement. Fingers seemed like thumbs as she twirled her hair into a loose chignon on top of her head.

There was a full moon shining down out of a cloudless sky, as she stepped out on to the verandah. 'Come to my room,' Adam had told her. She moved quickly along past Nurse Lee's

window. For some unknown reason she didn't
want to be seen going along to the surgeon's
quarters. It could easily be misconstrued . . .

Adam's windows were wide open and he was
leaning on the verandah rail, looking at the
moon. Her heart missed a beat and she caught
her breath. He looked so handsome in the
moonlight in his white tuxedo jacket. Much too
smart for her! Where on earth was he taking
her, for heaven's sake!

'Ah, there you are. I thought you'd got lost.'
He was smiling down at her, but he seemed
uneasy.

'I couldn't decide what to wear. I hope this is
OK.' Charlotte scanned the rugged features
anxiously for his reaction.

'You look charming.' What else could he say?
Wherever had she got those clothes? But her
hair was her redeeming feature; positively
stunning, in fact. If only he hadn't booked a
table at the Hilton! He could always ring up and
cancel . . .

'Where are you taking me?'

The trusting blue eyes were staring up into
his. How could he be so callous? he told himself.
'I thought it would be nice to go over to Hong
Kong Island and see the bright lights.' He took
hold of her arm and steered her along towards
the front of the hospital. 'Our boat's waiting.'
He breathed a sigh of relief as they escaped
through the gates. No one had seen them! The
rumours wouldn't start flying. He prided himself
on remaining uninvolved. Emotional attachments
had a habit of getting in the way of his
professional life, and work was all-important to
him.

The launch was bobbing gently in the harbour amid the variegated fishing vessels. Jim, the young Chinese boatman, smiled a bright, white-toothed grin and held out a hand to the new nurse, thinking how pretty she looked. Not as sophisticated as the women Dr Forster usually escorted, but infinitely more approachable and human. He untied the mooring rope and eased the boat out between the fishing boats and sampans, towards the mysterious stretch of black water between Cheung Lau and Hong Kong Island.

A cool, welcome breeze ruffled Charlotte's hair as the boat sped across the water. She watched in fascination as the flashing neon lights of Hong Kong grew ever nearer. As they pulled into Victoria Harbour she was amazed at the bustling activity on the waterside. It seemed like the middle of the day. In a daze she wandered along the front, aware of the comforting feel of Adam's fingers on her elbow, and the soothing sound of his rich, deep voice, as he explained where they were.

'This area is known as the Poor Man's Nightclub. We could have dined here at one of the noodle stalls, but I thought it would be more fun to live it up.'

She nodded, still bewildered by the multifarious activities around her. A group of dancers were performing intricate dance steps in a clearing in the crowd; further away a singer was singing a loud, strident, haunting melody.

'I tell your fortune, madame.' A small, yellow-skinned man in an exotic robe plucked at the sleeve of her blouse with his gnarled fingers.

She backed off. 'No; no, thank you.'

'Come on, Charlotte, let the man tell your fortune. It's only a bit of fun. Everyone has it done, when they come here.' Adam was staring down at her in amusement. 'No need to take it seriously.'

'Madame will have many children.' The old man had taken hold of her hand, encouraged by Adam's words. 'She will have three tall sons, with golden hair . . .'

'Oh, stop it! Don't be so stupid!' Charlotte's anguished voice rang out amidst the elegant, relaxed onlookers.

Adam squirmed with embarrassment as he pressed some Hong Kong dollars into the fortune-teller's hand and hurried his belligerent companion through the crowd.

'What was all that about?' he muttered, as they reached the edge of the car park, on which the Poor Man's Nightclub took place.

Charlotte had recovered some of her composure. She had blinked back the tears and taken a few deep breaths as Adam marched her along in a vicelike grip.

'I hate having my fortune told.' She managed to make it sound light, even giving a little laugh. 'It's so absurd; I mean, he saw the colour of my hair, and immediately he starts talking about golden-haired sons. As if I could possibly . . .' Her voice trailed away as she saw the curious look on Adam's face.

'I don't see why not,' he muttered as he turned away to hail a cab.

The red taxi screeched to a halt in front of the Hilton and a uniformed doorman hurried forward to greet them. Charlotte stepped out, her knees trembling with trepidation. Why had she accepted this preposterous invitation? Adam Forster was much too sophisticated for her. She could see from the cool look on his face that he was regretting his impulsive gesture. They were light years apart in terms of experience. He'd travelled the world many times over, while she had been at home coping with the daily drudgery of sickness and domestication.

He took her arm and led her through the crowded foyer to the lift. As it flew up to the top floor she glanced at the well-dressed Chinese couple beside them. Yes, she would definitely ring Jane, on her next off duty, and go shopping.

She walked across the luxurious carpet into the large dining and dancing room. From the surrounding windows she caught a glimpse of the flashing iridescence of Hong Kong by night, far below them. A deferential waiter was ushering them to a corner table.

Thank goodness the lights are low, Charlotte was thinking, as she smoothed down her rustic skirt. She didn't know her escort was having exactly the same thoughts.

'What will you have to drink?'

She hesitated, staring up into the deep, enquiring blue eyes. 'Something not too strong,' was her vague reply.

Ye gods! What have I done to deserve this? Adam thought. Only myself to blame, I suppose. He flashed her a bright, false smile. 'We'll have a bottle of champagne,' he said to the waiter. 'The one I usually have.'

'Yes, sir.' The waiter hurried away approvingly. Only the best for Dr Forster. He was hoping they still had a bottle of his favourite champagne. If not, he'd have to send out for some. This was

one client who could not be fobbed off with an
indifferent champagne.

Charlotte took a tentative sip from the crystal
glass and the bubbles flew up her nose.
Unexpectedly she giggled, and Adam smiled his
approval.

'That's better; about time you relaxed. Here's
to a good working relationship.' He raised his
glass towards her and she followed suit, enjoying
the warm, rosy glow she felt when she looked
into his eyes.

'Shall we dance?' Might as well go the whole
hog, he was thinking, as he stood up.

She was surprisingly light on her feet and he
twirled her round the floor, enjoying the feel of
her lithe figure in his arms. She followed his
steps well, having no difficulty when he introduced
one or two variations of his own.

'Where did you learn to dance?' he asked, as
he swept her along past the band, in full
spotlight.

'At school.' Her laughter could be heard above
the loud music. She felt happy and carefree
again, heady with the rhythm of the music,
disturbed by the closeness of that hard, virile
body. It was a good thing she had learned to
dance when she was very young. What had the
gym mistress told her? 'You'll be able to know
what the gentleman is going to do next by the
position of his hips.' It had made her blush at
the time. She hadn't imagined she could ever
dance close enough to feel the position of the
hips, but it was true! And, contrary to her
thoughts as a young girl, it was positively
exhilarating, sending shivers from the top of her
spine down to her toes. She closed her eyes and

abandoned herself to the sensual swaying of the music, revelling in the smell of expensive aftershave, and the contact with taut, rippling muscles.

When the dance ended, Adam led her back to her seat and took a drink of his champagne. What a strange girl, he mused. She really came to life out there on the dance floor. I could feel her moving in my arms as if she loved every second. He glanced at her flushed face, admiring the even pearly teeth as she smiled up at him. Perhaps it would be a good evening, after all.

'Would you like to order now?' He handed her a menu.

It looked more like a cookery book. Where should she start? 'I'm not too sure what I'd like,' she began, scanning the pages hopefully.

'If I might suggest . . .'

'Oh, please do!' Charlotte listened, enthralled, as he gave her a guided tour of the different kinds of food available in Hong Kong. There was Chinese, Cantonese, Peking, Shanghai, Szechuan, Chiu Chou, Hakka . . . She was hopelessly confused by now and freely admitted it.

Adam gave her a tender smile. She was an appealing little thing when she let her hair down, metaphorically speaking, that was. He glanced at the shining blonde strands piled on top of her head, feeling a sudden urge to tear out the constricting pins and run his fingers through it.

'We'll have shark's fin soup,' he said quickly. 'And Peking duck with spring rolls and mixed vegetables.'

'Very good sir.' The waiter topped up the eminent doctor's glass, noticing that the young lady had hardly touched hers. He hadn't seen her with Dr Forster before. Must be new out here.

'So, how's the broken heart?'

Charlotte looked startled at his unexpected question, but then, remembering their silly game on the beach, she smiled. 'It's healing,' she replied softly. Oh, if he only knew!

'Good. No man is ever worth crying over. You've got to forget the past and look forward, Charlotte. You've got all your life in front of you.'

A wretched tear lurked in the corner of her eye. Oh, why doesn't he shut up! she wanted to scream, but instead she forced herself to smile at him.

Adam noticed her sadness. My God, he thought, she must have been hurt badly! How could anyone do that to such a vulnerable young thing? He felt protective towards her, as he reached out his arm and took her hand in his. 'Want to talk about it?' he asked softly.

She shook her head, not trusting herself to speak, but her hand remained motionlessly imprisoned within his firm, comforting grasp. If only she could have met him sooner, when there was more time. A couple of years would have constituted a lifetime with a man like this. Was this what they meant by falling in love? This warm, helpless glow, spreading throughout the entire body, making you feel that nothing else mattered but to be near the one you loved. Gently she extricated her fingers, afraid that Adam would notice the profound effect he was having upon her.

The food had arrived and the waiter was solemnly ladling the soup out into delicate china dishes. Charlotte watched, fascinated, as the thick strands folded themselves into the strange-looking liquid. Her appetite had returned and she took some soup into her spoon. It was delicious!

Adam watched, amused at her obvious pleasure. He was glad to see she had a healthy appetite. It was awful to take someone out to dinner who picked at their food.

They finished off with tea, served in wafer-thin cups.

'Would you like your usual brandy, sir?' The waiter was hovering obsequiously.

'Not tonight. I'm on call, but you can bring me one of your best Havanas.' Adam grinned boyishly at Charlotte. 'I like to indulge myself, after an excellent dinner. Can I get you anything else?'

She shook her head. 'No, thanks. I've really enjoyed my meal. I think I'm going to like being here in Hong Kong.'

He marvelled at her direct response and childlike enthusiasm. 'Did you say your parents had died recently?' he asked gently, not wanting to disturb the precious rapport that had been building up between them during the evening.

'Yes. My mother had been ill for many years, and my father died soon after the funeral. It's ages since I've been anywhere interesting.'

'That would account for it.' He hadn't meant to sound patronising, but he noticed her puzzled look.

He must think I'm such a country mouse, she thought as she watched the clouds of blue smoke curling upwards from his expensive cigar. I bet he never asks me out again. She sighed.

'Tired?'

'No; I'm fine,' she replied hastily, wanting the night to go on for ever.

'Tell me about yourself.' Adam was intrigued by her. She was so different from anyone he had ever taken out before; so fresh, so untouched; but there was an air of mystery about her that he wanted to dispel. He had a very enquiring mind.

'There's nothing to tell,' Charlotte answered quickly. 'I started my nursing training at St Catherine's, and left after two years to look after my mother and help Daddy with the practice. The last few years have been deadly dull . . .'

She broke off as she saw the compassionate look on his face. He held out his hand as the music started again. It was a slow, romantic waltz. 'Let's dance,' he said simply.

She felt as if she were in a dream as he guided her round the floor. The feel of his strong arms holding her sent spasms of ecstasy through her body. She had never felt like this before. If only it could go on for ever . . .

'Calling Dr Adam Forster! Will Dr Forster please go to the nearest phone?'

Charlotte gave a start as the message came over the tannoy, drowning the poignant melody. Abruptly Adam stopped, and his arms dropped to his sides.

'Wait for me at the table.' It was a brusque command from her boss, who was putting her in her place once more.

She did as he asked, drumming her fingers on the starched white cloth. It had been an idyllic interlude, but she had known it couldn't last. Nothing ever did.

The tall, athletic figure hurried away from her and disappeared, but not before she had noticed the admiring glances of the cosmopolitan clientele. 'Isn't that *the* Dr Forster, the famous surgeon?' she heard someone ask. 'I didn't know he was out here. Last time I read about him, he was in Africa. Gets around, doesn't he!' She was aware of the enquiring glances, and knew they would all be thinking that she wasn't his type.

Minutes passed, but it seemed like hours before he reappeared. 'We've got to go,' he announced brusquely. 'There's a helicopter standing by.'

Charlotte's eyes widened in amazement. 'A helicopter? Here at the Hilton?'

'Oh, don't be so naïve!' He took her arm impatiently, and almost pulled her through the curious onlookers.

She breathed a sigh of relief as the swing doors closed after them and he relaxed his grip. They made for the lift. A car was waiting out front with a police escort. Charlotte hurried inside, not daring to ask questions, for fear of sounding more stupid than she felt.

The strange cortège zoomed through the night-time revellers and tore up the steep road to the Peak, in a cacophony of wailing sirens. She felt very small and frightened. Suddenly Adam's hand was on hers and she turned to look at him gratefully. The strong, multi-coloured neon lights were casting brilliant shadows across his face, making his eyes brighter than usual.

'You remember Mr Jiang, the patient with athero-sclerosis?'

She frowned, searching back over the patients she had looked after. There was a Mr Jiang . . .

'You gave him a bed-bath,' he snapped irritably.

'Oh, you mean the cardiac arrest.'

Adam rolled his eyes upwards. 'God give me strength!' he muttered, through clenched teeth, before he began his explanation in a more patient manner. For a while he had forgotten that Charlotte was not fully trained. He should be glad she knew as much as she did.

'After his cardiac arrest, we did a coronary angiogram to ascertain the extent of the athero-sclerosis. We found that the extent of the lesion was suitable for surgery, so we've been preparing him for a major operation. It was to have taken place next week at St Margaret's, but he's had another arrest. It's a case of life or death now, and we can't move him over from Cheung Lau. So . . .' he smiled at her resignedly, 'the mountain must come to Mahomet.'

'You mean you're going to take a surgical team across to our little theatre?' she asked incredulously.

'Exactly!'

'But won't that be a bit risky?'

'Yes. But it would be more of a risk to try and move the patient.'

They had reached the Peak hospital and were driving at breakneck speed to the helicopter pad. Helpful arms pulled Charlotte inside, and the weird whirring noise signalled that they were airborne. Far below, she could see the tiny pinpoints of light from the sea vessels. They swooped, perilously close, to the tall skyscrapers before heading out across the West Lamma Channel towards Cheung Lau.

The whole journey took only minutes. She had barely time to notice who was in the surgical team. A couple of Sisters bowed their heads in consultation with Adam and two other doctors. Mark Frobisher was one of them, and he smiled briefly at Charlotte before giving all his attention to the task in hand. Adam turned suddenly and spoke quietly to her.

'You might as well listen in to this. Some of it will be over your head, but you might learn something.'

She moved forward, pleased to be included. He was right; some of it was incomprehensible, but she gathered that he planned to dissect a section of the superficial saphenous vein from the patient's leg, and graft it on to the ascending aorta, bypassing the stenosis, and on to the coronary artery. At least there was nothing wrong with her anatomy and physiology when she rubbed away some of the rust.

'This will allow adequate perfusion of the myorcardium once again,' Adam finished off. 'I hope you will make allowances for our inferior theatre, ladies and gentlemen, but under the circumstances . . .'

There were murmurs of approval. 'Don't worry, old chap; we're right behind you.' 'Only thing we could do . . .'

One of the doctors had been sitting quietly listening. Charlotte had assumed, correctly, that he was the anaesthetist. He smiled at her sympathetically when the briefing was over.

'This your first time out here?'

She nodded. 'It's all rather confusing.'

'I'm sure it must be.'

She liked the way his mouth turned up at the corners. He looked about thirty, or maybe a little older. His mid-brown hair fell over his forehead in a delightful confusion, and she noticed his sensitive, expressive hazel eyes. He was the one who had helped her out of the helicopter when they touched down. Her legs had turned to jelly during the rapid, noisy descent, and she had flashed him a grateful smile.

'Thanks very much. I needed some assistance.' She leaned for a moment on his arm, before she set off across the field to the hospital. He fell into step beside her.

'We haven't been introduced, amidst all the drama. I'm Charles Gordon.'

'Charlotte Craven.'

'Will you be assisting in theatre?'

She laughed. 'I wouldn't imagine so for one moment!'

'There's no reason why you shouldn't scrub up and watch,' Adam put in, coming up quietly behind them.

'Oh, may I?'

Again, Adam thought how childlike she was, but her naïvety was not totally without appeal. It looked as if Charles found her attractive, anyway. 'Yes, but don't get in the way,' he replied gruffly, hurrying to the front of the little procession.

Sister Benson met them in Reception. 'Everything is ready for you, sir.'

Adam gave a curt nod and strode past her towards the theatre. Charlotte had fallen to the rear, feeling suddenly scared and insignificant.

'Where are you going, Nurse Craven?' asked Sister, not unkindly.

'Dr Forster said I could watch, Sister.'

'Did he now? Well, don't get in his way,' she whispered with a smile. 'Keep on the sidelines, whatever you do.'

'Of course.' She wouldn't be so stupid as to antagonise the great man. Funny—she thought of him as two different people, a sort of split personality. There was the fabulous, warmhearted man who swam like a fish and danced divinely, and there was the cold, calculating surgeon who expected perfection from her.

There was an air of expectancy as she pushed open the swing doors and went into the antetheatre. The patient was already motionless on the trolley, waiting for the anaesthetist. Charlotte didn't like his colour, and he looked even more painfully thin than she remembered from his bed-bath. Adam was, understandably, tense as he paced the floor, waiting for the heart-lung machine to be erected. This would do the work of both heart and lungs while the action of the heart was stopped. He wondered, for one brief moment, if he had made the right decision in bringing the team over to Cheung Lau. But he dismissed his fears as quickly as they arose. Decisions once made, after considering all the facts, should not be reversed. Vacillation was not in his nature . . .

'We're ready for you, sir.'

It was a long, complicated operation. Charlotte found her attention wandering at times. The long hours of the night passed and still the team bent over the still figure on the table. She marvelled at their stamina. Her own was definitely flagging. The highlight of her working contribution was when she was sent forward with a glass of water for the surgeon, but Adam didn't even notice her as she held it to his lips.

'Wipe my forehead, Nurse,' he barked imperiously.

'Yes, sir.' She put the glass in her other hand and reached for a piece of gauze.

For an instant there was recognition in his eyes, as she mopped the damp brow, before the Theatre Sister from St Margaret's intervened.

'I'll do that, Nurse. You'd better move back— too many of us round the table.'

Charlotte returned to her place near the door. It was only just possible to make out what was happening, but she gathered that they were in the final stages. The coronary lesion had been bypassed. The next few hours were crucial if the patient was to survive.

Adam was insisting on supervising the sutures. He was not the sort of surgeon who left anything to chance. The difficult work was finished, but he stayed on till the end, offering comments and criticisms.

'I believe we have a temporary intensive care unit, Sister Benson?'

She nodded, her eyes above the mask shining proudly. It had been a complicated task, but everyone had pulled together to get it ready in time. And she had always wanted to use the apparatus.

'And is it adequately staffed?'

'Nurse Lee and Nurse Wong are standing by.'

'Good.' An excellent pair, those two, Adam thought, he would have no need to worry about first-class nursing care, but Mr Jiang's life still hung in the balance. He daren't go to bed that night—or rather what remained of it.

'He's all yours, Charles,' he said to the anaesthetist, pulling down his mask and making for the door. He smiled at Charlotte as she leaned wearily against the wall.

'Tired?' he asked, unnecessarily.

She nodded, but pulled herself away from the wall.

'Come and help me with this wretched gown, before you pass out entirely.'

Her heart missed a beat at his gentle tone. Her weariness forgotten, she followed him quickly out of theatre. He only had to crook a finger and she came running. What's happening to me? she thought as she fought to stop her pulses racing madly.

Her fingers trembled as she untied the strings at the back of the surgeon's gown. He stood patiently waiting until she had finished. The gown was damp with sweat as she peeled it from him and threw it in the bin.

'Thanks.' He tossed his cap in the same general direction. 'Do you think you could whistle up some coffee, Charlotte?'

Sister Benson glanced across sharply. 'Charlotte', was it now? He'd changed his tune about the new recruit all of a sudden! 'There's coffee in the common room, sir,' she said quickly.

'Good.' He went out through the swing doors, carrying his white tuxedo incongruously over his arm. Everyone was wondering where he could possibly have been.

Charlotte hugged the secret to herself, remembering the feel of those sensitive arms around her as they danced . . .

'You'd better get some sleep, Nurse Craven,' Sister Benson said, taking an extra long look at the new nurse. There's more in her than meets the eye, she was thinking shrewdly.

Charlotte moved off, as in a dream. When she lay in the narrow bed her thoughts began to jump around, making it impossible to sleep. It had been a long and difficult operation, but there was every chance that it would be successful, that Mr Jiang's heart would function normally again. So why was it that in her own case surgery was inadvisable? She searched her mind for the exact words of the report. Yes, that was what it had said. 'Surgery is inadvisable at the present time . . .' Did that mean that they hadn't yet discovered a cure for her particular abnormality, or possibly that her health was too precarious, or what? If only I hadn't thrown away the piece of paper! she thought. What an idiot! It would be wonderful if Adam could perform an operation to keep her alive. Oh, she did so want to live now!

But it was silly to even contemplate it. She'd have another check-up when she went home in three months' time. Julia would have finished her finals by then, and whatever the outcome, she wouldn't be so much of a burden.

CHAPTER FIVE

IT was difficult to believe that a whole month had passed by. Charlotte swung down the hospital corridor with a new-found confidence. She was learning something every day and building up a store of medical information as well as adding to her expertise in general nursing care. Added to the fact that she had never felt fitter, life was pretty good! True, she would have liked to have gone out with the great surgeon again, but she hadn't expected him to ask for a repeat engagement. He must have recognised that she was not his type. He'd only been feeling sorry for her.

She pushed open the doors of the medical section. Mr Jiang had made an excellent recovery from his operation and had been returned to his old bed—or rather chair, at the moment. Charlotte smiled as she saw him sitting jauntily by the window.

'You're looking well today.'

The Oriental features creased into a welcoming grin. 'I velly good,' he pronounced happily. 'Prenty velly good.'

Charlotte placed her fingers on his wrist, searching for the now healthy pulse. His English is about as good as my Cantonese, she thought wryly—probably better! It wasn't easy to find

73

time every day to work with her cassettes and grammar book, but still she struggled on.

'You go Festival?' he asked.

'What festival?' Charlotte reached for Mr Jiang's thermometer and shook it down.

'Dragon Boat Festival,' he announced carefully.

'You can watch it from down in the harbour,' Nurse Lee called from across the room. 'We have one every year on the fifth day of the fifth moon. It's very spectacular. Crowds of oarsmen in long, thin dragon boats race to the beat of big bass drums.'

'Sounds fascinating. Why do they do this?'

'It's supposed to commemorate the tragic watery death of an ancient Chinese statesman-poet called Chu Yuan, who threw himself into a river to protest against corruption. Fishermen, in an effort to save him from flesh-eating fish, threw rice cakes into the river and beat the water with their boat paddles.'

'I'm on duty till five,' Charlotte told her.

'Pity; you'll miss the best bit. Still, it's worth going down afterwards. The atmosphere is so exciting!' Suzie Lee's eyes shone with anticipation. 'I shall be there. I've got a half day.' Her years of nursing training in London had not diminished her enthusiasm for the Chinese festivals. Quite the reverse; she loved Hong Kong passionately, and, in particular, Cheung Lau where she had been born. 'I'll save you a place in the crowd.'

'Thanks.' Charlotte was ever grateful to Suzie for the help she had given her through those first weeks. She didn't know what she would have done without her. Once or twice she had almost confided her deadly secret to her, but had stopped short at the last moment. It wasn't fair to worry her, and besides, she didn't want to be treated any differently. She filled in Mr Jiang's TPR chart and reached for the sphygmomanometer.

I've come a long way, she was thinking, as she pumped up the rubber bag. Sister Chen had been totally opposed to her taking blood pressures at first, but gradually her resistance had been broken down, as she realised the extent of Charlotte's experience. She listened with her stethoscope over the brachial artery, noting the level of the column of mercury at the first sound of the returning pulse. Carefully she reduced the cuff pressure and smiled reassuringly at her patient.

'Excellent, Mr Jiang. Very good,' she added, in case 'excellent' was not in his vocabulary. 'You're doing splendidly.' As she bent to write up the result on the chart, she sensed that someone was behind her.

'You're not doing too badly yourself.'

The surgeon was smiling his approval as she turned to look at him. To her embarrassment, she blushed. This was the first time he had praised her work. Criticisms she was used to and could handle, but compliments—that was a different matter!

'Sister Benson has been asking if you could help out in the surgical unit,' Adam told her, 'They're rather busy at the moment. I said I didn't see why not, and Sister Chen is willing to release you.'

I bet she is! thought Charlotte. Probably can't wait to get rid of me! She looked up into the searching blue eyes and the now familiar feeling

flooded through her again. Why did he have to
look so devastatingly handsome? Even in his
white coat—or especially in his white coat. She
drew in her breath sharply. 'I'll come at once.'
She felt positively important!

He held open the door in a gallant gesture
and then fell into step beside her. 'Sister
particularly wanted you to help out with
dressings,' he said.

She smiled happily. At last she really was
accepted! 'That will be fine. I spent a lot of time
on dressings in my father's surgery,' she told
him.

'Did you ever have to remove stitches?'

'Of course!' She glanced up at him quickly,
not wanting to sound as if she were boasting,
but she'd probably removed more stitches than
he had. Surgeons were expert at putting stitches
in but had little practice in taking them out.

He grinned and patted her arm. 'Quite the
little Florence Nightingale!'

Charlotte quickened her step. Why did he
always have to be so patronising!

'Ah, Nurse Craven, I'm glad you've arrived.'
Sister Benson came hurrying down the surgical
unit to meet them. 'You told me the other day
you had had some experience on the surgical
ward at St Catherine's and in general practice,
so I thought I'd put you to the test. I'll supervise
you during your dressings round for the first
session, although, heaven knows, I'm rushed off
my feet today . . .'

'You carry on with your own work, Sister. I'll
go round with Nurse Craven,' said the surgeon
quietly.

'Oh, I didn't mean to put the onus on you, sir . . .' Sister began.

'That's OK. She is my responsibility, after all. Where's the list?'

Sister went over to her desk while Charlotte fetched the trolley from the sterilising room. Her fingers trembled as she checked over the instruments, and her legs felt weak at the knees as they approached the first patient.

'This is Mr Pak, Nurse. I did a partial gastrectomy at the beginning of last week. Let's have a look at the wound, shall we.' He launched into fluent Cantonese and the patient smiled broadly, glancing nervously at Charlotte.

I wonder what he's saying about me, she thought anxiously. Probably told him I'm a complete novice. She pulled back the covers and placed a dressing sheet over the abdomen. When she had removed the soiled dressing, she went over to the sink to scrub up, aware that Adam was watching her out of the corner of his eye, as he chatted amiably with the patient.

She picked up the sterile forceps and held the suture in one hand, snipping it quickly with sterile scissors. It came away easily, not snagging or pulling or any of the other hazards she had anticipated as she had scrubbed her hands.

The patient smiled happily, and said something to the doctor.

'Mr Pak says he didn't feel a thing,' Adam translated, his eyes showing his approval of her technique.

'I'm glad about that.' Charlotte didn't look up from her work. Best not to get too complacent. It wasn't finished yet . . .

'OK, you can relax now. You're much too tense.'

She straightened her back as the last stitch came away. Well, if that was his only criticism, she was perfectly happy! He was glancing down the list of dressings.

'I'll have a look at Mr Ho's drainage tube, but after that you'll be OK on your own. Sister's within earshot, if you run into something you can't handle, but I don't foresee any problem.'

As he left her, he leaned across and placed a hand on her shoulder, and she stiffened at the feel of his fingers. He obviously had no idea how he was affecting her, as he looked earnestly down.

'Keep it up! We'll make a trained nurse of you yet.'

She smiled up at him bravely, not daring to speak. Again he noticed the underlying sadness in her eyes. She puzzled him; he seemed unable to get through to her. There was some indefinable barrier which he could never penetrate. Even after their night out at the Hilton he had no idea what it was that made her tick—much less who it was who had hurt her. Perhaps he should take her out again. True, she wasn't his type, but she was intelligent and interesting to talk to . . .

'Are you going to watch the Dragon Boat Festival today?' he asked quietly.

'I can't get away till this evening.' This was the first time he'd shown an interest in her private life since she first arrived.

'Neither can I, but it's worth going down to the harbour. There'll be lots going on.'

'So I'm told.'

'I'll take you down there, if you like,' he offered. 'It's always rather crowded.'

'Suzie Lee said she would save me a place, but . . .'

'That's OK, then; hope you enjoy it.' He turned away and went out through the swing doors.

Why did I open my big mouth? Charlotte thought crossly. Suzie would have understood if I'd turned up with Adam. She bent over the patient cursing inwardly. Will I never learn? she asked herself. For a whole month he's ignored me. I was beginning to think he found me repulsive or something, and now . . .

'Is that comfortable, Mr Ho?' she switched her attention quickly, as she closed the dressing.

The patient nodded gratefully, thinking what a nice, gentle nurse she was. Calmer than the girl who'd dressed him yesterday. 'What is your name?' he asked carefully, proud of his command of the English language. His children might laugh at his poor accent; they'd spent more hours in school already than he had, but he always managed to make himself understood in the end.

'Charlotte Craven.' She smiled down at the worried face. He was an unusually pallid man, having spent a long time in hospital after his bronchiectasis.

'I call you Charlotte.' He made an extra special effort to pronounce the difficult name.

'Please do.' She hoped Sister Benson wouldn't mind the familiarity. She was reputedly less stuffy than Sister Chen, even though she was Senior Sister, in charge of the hospital.

When Charlotte went to the dining room at

lunch time she felt pleased with her morning's work. She was actually getting somewhere, at long last! The lunch was excellent as usual and she managed to convey her approval to Mary, the cook, in Cantonese. Mary was something of a legend now in hospital circles. The larger hospital, St Margaret's, had tried to lure her over to the Peak, with promises of higher wages, but she refused to leave her family on Cheung Lau—fortunately for the staff of the smaller hospital. She cooked mainly Cantonese and Peking dishes, with the occasional foray into European cuisine, and everyone agreed she was a gem. Charlotte had no idea what her real name was. Jane had told her it was unpronounceable; she was always called Mary.

Charlotte put down her chopsticks, unable to eat another morsel of seafood or fried chicken. It had taken a while to learn to use chopsticks, but she had at last got the hang of it, and now actually preferred them. She took a sip of the fragrant jasmine tea. This was the life! she thought, checking a stray notion in her head, nagging about how long she could go on like this before . . .

Throughout the afternoon, the sound of the activities in the harbour drifted in through the open windows of the hospital, making the patients restless and demanding. Charlotte could hear the incessant beating of the paddles on the water and the constant drone of the drums. As soon as she came off duty she changed into a cool cotton skirt and blouse and hurried down to the sea.

'Over here!' Suzie Lee was waving to her madly from her vantage point on a stone monument, and Charlotte pushed her way through the goodnatured crowd. Friendly hands reached forward to help her climb up beside her friend.

'It's been so exciting—there's the winning boat coming in now!'

Charlotte looked at the long, slim canoe, hollowed out of wood. The front was shaped like a dragon's head with the mouth wide open to reveal a bright red tongue and startling white teeth. Palm fronds waved precariously from the nostrils, completing the garish caricature. The crowd cheered enthusiastically and the drums beat ferociously, adding to the mounting exuberance.

Suddenly a hush fell on the crowd. Round the corner of the harbour, a frail, overcrowded fishing boat had appeared. Its wooden hulk was split in several places; some of the people on board were frantically baling out water. It seemed that at any moment it would sink, and its pathetic human cargo with it.

'Refugees,' Suzie whispered. 'They won't be allowed to land.'

'But they can't be turned away!' Charlotte stared out at the pitiful sight.

There must have been at least forty people herded together in the boat, men, women and children. Even from this distance she could see their emaciated bodies and ragged clothing. The music had stopped; there was an eerie silence broken only by the poignant wailing of the approaching refugees.

Down in the harbour, a khaki-clad figure was pushing his way importantly to the front. Sergeant Leung knew what his orders were. No refugees on Cheung Lau. They were to go straight to the army camps in the New Territories. Didn't they have enough problems without having to absorb these unwanted escapees? He reached the water side and waved his arms, angrily shouting something unintelligible to Charlotte. But, from the tone of his voice, it wasn't difficult to imagine what he was saying.

Charlotte jumped down to the ground. 'Come on, Suzie! We've got to do something. That policeman's insane! Those people will drown if we don't take them in.' She pushed through the murmuring crowd, spurred on by new-found energy, and reached the harbour at the same time as a familiar figure.

Adam hadn't even stopped to remove his white coat when the news of the approaching refugee boat had reached him. He was panting for breath as he argued vociferously with Sergeant Leung. 'They must be allowed to land! I don't care what your orders are, we've got to take them in and care for them initially. Look at the state of that boat! I'm surprised it's got this far.'

'I cannot allow . . .'

'I'll telephone your superior this evening. Now, get out of my way!'

The policeman backed off when he heard Adam's threatening tone. Realising that there was no stopping the angry surgeon, he turned away smartly, and went back to his office to put in a call to the inspector in Hong Kong.

'Thank goodness you're here!' Adam smiled at Charlotte and Suzie. 'We're going to need all the help we can get.'

Sister Benson was pushing her way through. 'I've asked for some stretchers,' she said tersely.

'Good. Looks like we're going to need them.'

Adam ran a hand through his tousled fair hair and stared out at the refugees. Was there no end to the problems? He leaned forward anxiously, as the boat creaked alongside the harbour, threatening to spill its load into the sea. A rope was thrown and secured, and then the task of disembarking the refugees began. Many simply leapt overboard and swam to shore, unable to contain their relief at reaching land— any land! After the ordeal they had been through, to be alive was miraculous. But the ill and injured lay quietly and submissively in the bottom of the boat waiting for whatever fate had in store for them now. Since leaving Vietnam they had experienced every kind of deprivation. Of the five boats which had originally set out so hopefully, this was the only one that remained.

Terrible tragedies had been played out unseen off the coast of Thailand where fishermen-turned-pirates had plundered the helpless refugees, murdering, raping and abducting at will. A violent storm had claimed four of the boats, which simply fell apart, because they were unseaworthy. Some people had died of thirst, some of hunger, but this handful had survived. They had no money, no possessions, but they were alive.

The next few hours were a harrowing experience for Charlotte. She helped to transport the ones who couldn't walk up to the hospital on an endless chain of stretchers. Adam asked for volunteer stretcher bearers from the crowd, to relieve the medical staff for more urgent duties. Every bed was soon filled and makeshift cots were set up in the corridors and every available space.

They were quickly divided into those who needed specialist medical attention and those who merely required general nursing care to alleviate the malnutrition.

Charlotte found herself assigned to take care of the latter category. She didn't mind. It was better to let the trained staff get on with the difficult work. Besides, it was completely satisfying to see the look of wonder on the refugees' faces when she produced the bowls of rice. They scrabbled at them with eager fingers, licking the remains with their tongues to make sure they didn't miss any. She cuddled a tiny scrap of a girl in her arms and tried to spoon some food into her. She didn't appear to belong to anyone. Perhaps her mother had perished on the journey, or she might have paid out money for her daughter to be taken to the promised land.

The child grizzled quietly, showing no interest in the food. She had gone past the stage where hunger meant anything to her. I'll have to get her on a glucose saline drip until she's stronger, Charlotte thought, otherwise she'll simply slip away into a coma and die. She carried the child through into the reception area. Adam was trying to cope with several cases at once and snapped at her when she tried to get his attention.

'What is it, Nurse? Can't you see I'm up to my eyes?'

'We shall lose this one if something isn't done quickly.' She spoke quietly and firmly.

He glanced across at the little girl in Charlotte's arms, his practised eye noticing the greying skin and utter lethargy.

'Put a cot over by that wall. I'll set up an IV.'

She moved quickly. The cots were all in use, but she found a mattress and covered it hurriedly with a sheet, before laying her pathetic little patient on it.

Adam's face was tense, but he relaxed for a few moments to smile at the child. There was no response from the glazed eyes. She didn't move as the cannula was inserted and the life-giving fluid began to flow into her veins.

'Keep an eye on her. With any luck . . .' The surgeon was already moving away, but he stopped briefly and took a long hard look at Charlotte. Maybe she could help him with this difficult case. She seemed to have a way with children. 'Can you give me a hand for a moment?'

She looked up from her patient in surprise. 'Of course.' She had already splinted the tiny arm—not that there was much danger of the girl moving it. She followed Adam across the room and into a curtained-off cubicle. As she looked at the young boy lying on the stretcher, she stifled a cry of horror.

The foot and lower limb of one leg were mutilated beyond recognition. Charlotte raised her eyes to the surgeon's.

'A shark,' he said quietly. 'The pirates threw him into the sea after robbing and killing his parents. I gather that he clung on to a piece of wood until he was picked up by the other boat. His older brother was with him. The sharks preferred him.'

She felt a cold shiver run through her body as she gazed at the plucky survivor. The narrow eyes stared back beseechingly. She averted her attention from the gory limb, but Adam spoke sharply.

'Hold his knee, will you? I'm going to put a sterile dressing on the worst bits, and then I'll take him down to theatre for an amputation.'

'It can't be saved, then?'

He shook his head. 'Gas gangrene has set in. If I move quickly I can save the upper limb and do a simple below-knee amputation. With a prosthesis, he'll walk again.' He spoke gently to the boy as he dressed the leg.

Charlotte held on to the knee. The boy seemed to be in considerable pain, but he smiled bravely as Adam explained what he was going to do. Suddenly she realised she was understanding what Adam was saying. He was speaking in French—one of her best subjects at school! Of course, the boy came from Vietnam, and many of the Vietnamese could speak French, especially the younger ones. She smiled down at him. At last she could make herself understood.

'*Comment t'appelles-tu*?' she asked softly.

'Wing Tai,' came the whispered reply.

'What a lovely name!' She grasped the boy's hand affectionately.

Adam flashed her a grateful smile. 'Stay with Wing Tai until I get back, and keep him talking— if you can,' he added with a sympathetic grin. 'I want to get things moving in theatre.'

He was back within minutes carrying a kidney dish and a syringe. 'Give him this pre-med.' He went out again.

Charlotte swabbed the skinny arm. '*Quel âge as-tu*?' she asked to keep his mind off the injection.

'*Dix ans*,' he replied in a barely audible voice.

Only ten years old! And to have suffered so much. She pressed on the syringe. Adam returned with Sister Benson.

'I'm going to do a below-knee amputation, Sister.'

She nodded. 'Dr Gordon is on his way over from St Margaret's. He'll be here any minute.'

Even as she spoke, they heard the whirring of the helicopter overhead. 'Dr Frobisher is coming along to take charge while we're in theatre, and he's bringing some more nurses,' said Sister.

'Good.'

'I'll go back to my other little patient and check on the IV,' Charlotte said.

Sister smiled at her. 'That's the way, Nurse!'

When Charlotte had gone Helen Benson turned to the surgeon and said, 'Useful little nurse, that one.'

'Better than I expected,' was his brief reply.

The little girl had opened her eyes and was looking round warily. She gave a cry of recognition as Charlotte bent over her. This was a face she had seen before in this strange place. She tried to move her arm, but something was holding it down. Her eyelids felt heavy, so she let them droop. It was so much easier to sleep on and on . . .

Charlotte put a pillow under the tiny head and adjusted the arm to a more comfortable position. Mark Frobisher was striding across the large room with Charles Gordon, followed in hot pursuit by four nurses. Sister Benson went to meet them.

'Take over in here, Nurse,' she called to Charlotte.

Charlotte went back into the cubicle and

looked down at the solemn face of Wing Tai.
The premedication was beginning to take effect.
Some of the tenseness had vanished from his
young features and it was obvious that he felt
less pain. She stayed quietly by his side simply
holding his hand. At one point, when a spasm
of pain got through, he gripped her fingers
tightly and then relaxed as the drug took effect.

By the time Sister came back, he was asleep.
'Two of the nurses from St Margaret's are going
to help you with feeding and drinks,' Sister told
Charlotte. 'Then you'd better settle the patients
down as best you can. It won't be easy. We're
hopelessly overcrowded, but St Margaret's can't
take any of them because of the political
complications.'

Charlotte looked puzzled. 'Could you
explain . . .'

'Not now, Nurse, there isn't time. Dr Forster
is waiting in theatre. Help me push this trolley.
Don't know where that porter's got to!'

The swing doors of the theatre had closed and
Charlotte felt worried for her little patient as she
left him in the hands of the theatre staff. Still,
they were a good team—and the surgeon was
the best there was. She mustn't become too
involved with her patients. Got to remain
professional . . .

It was ten o' clock before the patients had all
been seen and settled into some semblance of a
bed. Charlotte sat on the edge of a mattress
comforting a young rape victim. The girl herself
hadn't told them about it, but one of the other
refugees, a motherly sort who had taken to
looking after her, had confided in Charlotte,
thinking she looked a nice sympathetic nurse.

Adam had nodded grimly when she told him, and coaxed the girl into an examination.

'No gynaecological complications at the moment,' he reported. 'She's been lucky.'

Lucky! thought Charlotte. Hardly how I would have described it. But she knew what he meant. The girl could have been badly mutilated, or even killed.

'Stay with her for a while, Charlotte, if you've time. She needs a female shoulder to cry on.'

He sounded tired. She glanced at his worried face, longing to smooth away some of the lines and see again the boyish face of the man who had plunged into the sea all those weeks ago.

'How's Wing Tai?' she asked gently.

'So far so good, but he's not out of the wood yet. I've still got him in Recovery.' He seemed to notice her for the first time since the refugees had arrived. 'You look tired, Charlotte.'

'I was thinking the same about you.'

He laughed softly and she felt relieved to see the relaxed contours of his face again. 'I'm used to this sort of thing, but it must be tough on you. Go off duty as soon as this patient is asleep. I've given her a sedative, so she'll be all right. The night staff are here.'

'But what about you?'

He smiled gently, the corners of his mouth moving slowly upwards, and his full, sensuous lips lazily uncovering the strong white teeth. 'All this concern for me is very touching. What's this? The maternal instinct?'

Charlotte bit back a retort. Couldn't he see that her concern was not in the least maternal? She turned away to smile at her patient. The girl was reaching out towards her and Charlotte took hold of her hand. She heard Adam's retreating footsteps but did not look round. The patient needed her; he didn't. He was complete in himself, wrapped up in his career . . .

The girl talked quietly to her, in a strange Vietnamese dialect. They had tried French, but it was too much effort for both of them. When the girl had fallen asleep, Charlotte tiptoed away, taking a last look at the tiny patient on the IV. She lay motionless on the mattress. Pray God she made it through the night . . .

CHAPTER SIX

For the next few days the refugees held all their attention. Normal off duty was cancelled and everyone worked for hours at a stretch, as the need arose. Charlotte found the pace hectic, but she was no more tired than anyone else. She began to wonder if there could possibly have been a mistake in her medical report. If she hadn't seen it with her own eyes she would never have believed it. After her parents' deaths she had felt so ill and confused. Maybe some of that was just a normal reaction to the ordeal she had been through? When she went back to the UK she determined to ask for a repeat of the medical tests. It was worth a try. She had nothing to lose, after all. Meanwhile, there was work to be done . . .

She smiled down at the tiny, emaciated girl in the newly changed sheets. Difficult to believe she was four years old—or so Adam had estimated. From the actual size of her, she looked about eighteen months. It was also difficult to believe that this was the lethargic creature they had put on a drip on that first evening. Charlotte was actually able to coax a little smile from her today!

'Yin Fen, are you hungry?' Charlotte lifted the little girl on to her lap. It was Suzie Lee who had decided on the name; all attempts at finding her real one had failed and Suzie thought the name suited her. She was a dear, elfin-like mite, with solemn brown eyes set in the olive skin. As yet she hadn't spoken a word in any language, but she appeared to be listening to all around her, and she jumped if there was a loud noise, so she couldn't be deaf. Might as well talk to her in English, Charlotte thought as she spooned in the rice into the eager mouth. She'll begin to understand me soon. Children learn languages very quickly at this age. Goodness, the bowl was nearly empty!

'What a clever girl you are!' she smiled.

'I could say the same about you.'

She looked up into the deep blue eyes, her heart thudding madly. 'Thank you, kind sir,' she quipped facetiously.

Adam smiled his heartrending smile. 'I mean it, Charlotte. You've been a great help. A valuable member of the team, if I may say so.'

Oh, you may! You may continue to praise me for as long as you like, so long as you'll just stand there looking down at me with those tender, expressive eyes. Charlotte cleared her throat.

'I'm glad I could be useful. It's been a great experience,' she said quickly.

'It will stand you in good stead during your eventual training. When do you plan to go back home?' He sounded frightfully professional and detached.

She swallowed hard. 'In about six weeks.'

'And what are your plans?' His eyes seemed to be boring inside her.

'Plans?' she repeated vacantly.

'What are you going to do when you return?' He couldn't keep the impatience from his voice. What on earth did she think he meant?

'I'm not sure . . .' she began guardedly.

'I mean, are you going to apply to a training school, because if you are . . .'

'I wish you'd stop asking questions!'

Adam stared at her in amazement. He had only wanted to help, to offer some advice and say that he would give her a reference if she needed it. She was actually choking back the tears! What had he said to upset her? He ran a hand through his hair. Women! He would never understand them. He understood their anatomy and physiology perfectly, but their psychology had always defeated him! For once in his proud life he would apologise.

'I'm sorry. I didn't mean to upset you.'

'And I'm sorry—I shouldn't have snapped like that. It's just that . . .'

'Yes?' he said hopefully.

Would he be able to help her? He was, after all, a brilliant heart surgeon . . . She paused, took a deep breath and then thought better of it. 'It's nothing, really,' she muttered.

'Well, I think you've been working too hard,' he announced, ever the helpful doctor with a recalcitrant patient. 'I'm going to prescribe a weekend off . . . no, don't argue.' He had raised his hand, as if to silence her protests.

'But what about the refugees?'

'No one is ever indispensable. Always remember that. Besides, they'll have to leave us soon.'

Charlotte stared at him in amazement. 'But where will they go?'

'Over to the army camp in the New Territories.'
His voice was cold and detached.

'But some of them aren't fit to be moved . . .'

'I know, but there's nothing we can do about
it. The current government policy is that no
more refugees can be absorbed into the colony.
They can't cope with any more. The social
services just won't stand it. So all refugees have
to go out to the camps . . .'

'But will they have medical facilities?'

Adam looked grim. 'They're adequate,' he
said quietly.

'Adequate!' She looked down at Yin Fen's
trusting little face. 'But surely we can keep the
children . . .'

'No! I can't break the rules,' he interrupted
firmly.

Charlotte looked at the strong rugged features.
Surely he could bend the rules a little, especially
for little Yin Fen? And what about Wing Tai?
Across the room, the little boy was swamped in
his bed by the orthopaedic cage over his stump.
He was making a remarkable recovery, but
now . . .

'Don't worry about it, Charlotte. It's my
problem, and like you, I prefer to find my own
solutions.' He turned away quickly, his face stern
and foreboding brooked no further discussion of
the matter. 'I'll see Sister Benson about that
weekend—and you must take it. That's an order.'

'Yes, sir,' she replied quietly and submissively,
but inside she was fuming. Surely a man like the
great Dr Adam Forster could do something!
There was a strange situation here on the small
island, she felt sure. She remembered Mai Ling,
the young girl who had given birth on that first

evening. Adam had said she couldn't stay. She had to go back. Back where? Where had he taken her? She remembered the horses' hooves in the night. Was there somewhere on the island—a haven for illegal refugees? If so, then Adam was taking an enormous risk, in the name of humanity. Mai Ling seemed to have vanished into thin air. No one had ever seen her again, and even Sister Benson refused to acknowledge her existence. Charlotte remembered how annoyed she had been when Sergeant Leung had asked if there had been any admissions.

'No admissions yesterday,' she had replied calmly. Well, that was true enough. Mai Ling had never been technically admitted. She had rested in Recovery for a couple of hours and then . . .

Then what? Charlotte puzzled. The little girl in her arms stirred restlessly, and put out a frail arm and touched her on the cheek.

'You've finished all your rice, Yin Fen, and I hadn't noticed! Do you want some more?'

'More!' repeated the little girl softly. It was the first word she had spoken since her arrival.

Charlotte hugged her. 'Oh, you wonderful child! Of course you shall have some more.' She carried Yin Fen over to the food trolley, on her hip, reluctant to break the precious rapport that was building up between them.

When the meal had been cleared away, she helped Nurse Lee with the dressings, watching in fascination as she made an expert bandaging of Wing Tai's stump. The little boy seemed to have accepted his lot with a stoicism beyond his years. Charlotte had no doubt that he would walk as soon as his prosthesis was fitted. But would there be skilled people to help him when he left here?

She pulled herself together. Adam had told her to stop worrying. It was his problem. She mustn't get involved.

'Ça va? Are you OK?' She smiled down at the brave little boy as she made his leg comfortable between sandbags.

'OK,' he pronounced with a grin, hoisting himself higher up his pillows with the pulley above his head.

He's as agile as a little monkey! she thought with relief. We'll have no complications here. She replaced the cradle over the stump and pulled up the covers.

'Do you want a drink?' She lifted up his water glass.

'Drink,' he repeated, holding out his hand. He swallowed half a glassful and licked his lips happily, remembering the times he had resorted to drinking the awful salty sea water, as he clung to a piece of wreckage, all alone in the big wide ocean, after his brother had disappeared in a swirl of blood and thrashing of fins. It was so good to be alive!

Charlotte patted him on the head affectionately and moved across the room, pushing the trolley. Suzie Lee went to scrub up while Charlotte removed the dressing from the patient's arm. There was a nasty cut running from elbow to wrist on the young woman's arm. Charlotte smiled down encouragingly at the young rape victim, feeling pleased with the progress she had made since that first evening.

'That looks healthy enough,' pronounced Suzie casting a practised eye over the healing tissue.

'Another dry dressing, I think. We'll soon be able to take the stitches out.'

The patient began to murmur in a gentle voice. She enjoyed talking to the nurses. Pity they don't understand me, she was thinking. But they smile at me, and they're so kind. I'm sure they must understand what I've been through. She closed her eyes for an instant as the full shock horror returned, momentarily, but then it was gone again. I mustn't think about it! In time I'll be able to forget. She began to speak her thoughts aloud to the two pretty nurses who were making her comfortable again, and they nodded, as if they knew what she was saying.

'Nurse Craven, may I have a word?'

'Of course, Sister Benson.' Charlotte hurried across to the beckoning figure.

'Dr Forster is concerned about your health and has asked me to give you a weekend off. It's long overdue; I don't usually work my nurses so hard, but we've had exceptional circumstances, as you must realise. I could spare you this weekend. St Margaret's has promised to help out with staffing. Make sure you have a good, relaxing time. Get right away from your work.'

'Yes, Sister.'

'What will you do? I don't mean to pry, but as you haven't been out here very long, it might be difficult to find your way around. If there's anything I can do to help . . .'

'That's OK, I'll ring my friend Jane,' Charlotte told her. 'I've been meaning to go over to see her.' It was a spontaneous decision. She hoped Jane wouldn't mind. Well, she had told her to go over any time, hadn't she?

Sister gave her a beaming smile. 'Of course—

I'd forgotten Jane was a friend of yours. I
remember when she first arrived out here. I was
still at St Margaret's then and Jane had been
appointed to take charge here. I remember
Matron introducing her to Dr Frobisher and they
both said they'd met before. We'd no idea just
how close they'd been! Oh, it was so romantic
when they got together again—after *eight years*!
I went to the wedding . . .

Charlotte glanced at the stars dancing in Helen
Benson's eyes. Another incurable romantic!
Aren't we all, she thought resignedly. Yes, it
would be good to see Jane again. Maybe she
would confide in her . . .

Jane was thrilled when she heard the sound of
Charlotte's voice on the phone. 'Of course you
can come for the weekend; and about time too!
I thought you'd got lost, but Mark explained
about the cancellation of off duty. How's
everything going?'

'Fine. I'll tell you more when I see you. Got
to dash.' Charlotte didn't want to go into details
on the phone. It was such an impersonal
instrument. Much better to have a cosy chat,
face to face.

She found herself getting excited as the
weekend approached, and when Saturday morning found her on the ferry going across to
Hong Kong Island she felt like a new person.
Adam had been right about the need to get
away from work, to stand back and view
things dispassionately, getting her problems into
perspective. The warm breeze was ruffling her
hair as she stared over the rail of the boat
towards the approaching land. It wasn't as
romantic as the last time she had pulled into

Victoria Harbour, with the handsome surgeon beside her.

She sighed, as she wondered what he had made of her that first evening. He must have found her deadly dull. She was sure she wasn't at all witty or interesting to be with, and as for her dress sense! She glanced down at her cotton trousers and the baggy shirt. I really must get Jane to take me on a shopping spree! she told herself.

The harbourside was crowded and noisy. Jane had told her to take a taxi; they were cheap and plentiful.

The taxi driver nodded his head knowingly. Yes, of course he knew the prestigious road where the Frobishers' house was situated. Didn't everyone in Hong Kong? He let in the clutch and screeched away up the road to the Peak.

Charlotte held her breath as the colourful scene swept past her. She could see the huge windows of the shops, displaying their wares. Vivid models stood motionless and inviting, in their up-to-the-minute creations. But the car swept past too quickly. She would have to return.

Jane came tearing out of the house when she heard the taxi. She had been worrying about her friend, wondering why she hadn't been over before. Surely she had made it clear that there was always a welcome in their home for her? But Charlotte had seemed strange and withdrawn when she had first arrived. It was nothing you could put your finger on, but she was determined to get to the bottom of it over the weekend.

'Charlotte!' She opened her arms and hugged

her. 'Goodness, you're skinnier than ever! Don't they feed you over on Cheung Lau?'

'The food's terrific! You should know that. But we've been rushed off our feet; haven't had time to put weight on. Anyway, I've decided to buy some new clothes, and who was it said you could never be too rich or too thin?'

Jane laughed and linked arms with Charlotte. This is more like the girl I used to know, she was thinking. 'Come inside. I've got some coffee waiting,' she smiled.

The morning passed quickly, both of them intent on trying to catch up on the news. Wai Yee, Jane's maid, looked after baby Samantha so that they could have an uninterrupted gossip.

'So you want to go shopping?' Jane looked quizzical. 'What brought this on? I thought you weren't interested in clothes.'

'Well, you must admit I haven't got a thing to wear!'

Jane smiled. 'The old cliché, but in your case, I think it's probably true. We'll go this afternoon. You've got to get something for tonight. I'm having a dinner party and I want everyone to see how pretty you can look out of uniform.'

Charlotte's pulses raced apprehensively. 'A dinner party—will it be terribly grand?'

'Good heavens, no! Just the usual crowd—anyone who can get off duty. It's time you met everyone socially for a change.'

Charlotte breathed deeply. 'Anyone who can get off duty'—would that include . . .? She daren't even think about it. No, he would be too busy at the hospital. Not a chance he would come. She didn't know whether she felt relieved or disappointed.

They had lunch in the nursery, sitting at a small table by the window overlooking the Bay of Hong Kong. Wai Yee served them with a delicious salad and huge king prawns, followed by fresh fruit and cheese. Samantha gurgled at them from her play mat on the floor, kicking her chubby little legs in the air. Towards the end of their meal, she started to become fractious.

'I'll have to feed her,' said Jane, getting up from the table. 'She's been very good, but I can tell when she's hungry. Come on, Samantha, lunchtime!' She picked up her daughter and settled in a comfortable nursing chair. 'Come over here, Charlotte. We can talk while I feed her. Wai Yee, would you bring the dish of baby food I prepared. It's in the kitchen, on the first shelf. Egg custard!' She pulled a face. 'This weaning business is so messy—half of it goes on the floor!'

Charlotte laughed as she watched mother and daughter. The breast-feeding part was highly satisfactory, but Samantha seemed to delight in blowing bubbles of egg custard over the edge of the spoon.

'OK, that's enough!' Jane put the bowl down. 'Time for your nap, my girl, and then Mummy's going for a little jaunt around the shops.'

As soon as the baby was settled, they left her in the capable hands of Wai Yee and set off down the Peak road in Jane's little car.

'We'll park in Central,' Jane decided. 'It's the best area for good fashions. It's possible to buy things from the open-air stalls, but you can never be sure of quality. That's one of my favourite shops. We'll come back to it when I've managed to park.'

Charlotte caught a glimpse of a prestigious
building. It looked expensive, but she didn't
mind. She'd brought lots of money out with her
and hadn't spent a thing. It would be easy to
cash some more travellers cheques or use her
credit cards. What did she need money for,
anyway? There was no point saving it up. Her
father had left her a sizeable legacy which she
hadn't touched yet. Eat, drink and be merry,
she thought gaily, for tomorrow . . .

They walked through the revolving door and
across the luxurious carpet.

'Mrs Frobisher, how lovely to see you!' A
small, exquisitely dressed lady in a Chinese hand-
embroidered gown hurried to meet them, between
the huge vases of expensive, delicately perfumed
flowers.

'Hello, Shu Qi. This is my friend Miss Craven.
We're looking for something a bit special for
evening wear—dinner parties and so on. You
know the sort of thing.'

The head saleswoman eyed the newcomer
critically. She's very skinny, she thought, but
that's not such a bad thing with the new cinched-
in waist. 'Sit down over here, ladies. Do
you prefer Chinese or Western fashions, Miss
Craven?'

'I don't mind. What do you think, Jane?'

'Show us a selection, Shu Qi, and we'll
choose.'

The older woman snapped her fingers and
spoke quickly to a couple of salesgirls, who
scuttled away to bring the required garments.

Charlotte had never spent such a fascinating
half hour buying clothes. It had always seemed
such a chore before. She chose a fabulous black

and white ballerina-length dress in filmy chiffon over taffeta.

'That's perfect! Turn round again.' Jane clapped her hands with delight at the transformation. 'Shoes! Have you got any shoes to wear with it?'

'Not really . . .'

'That means no.'

'If I might make a suggestion, madame . . .' Shu Qi had not been promoted to her exalted position for nothing. The superb kid high-heeled sandals she produced were a perfect match.

'I'll have them.' Charlotte was feeling completely reckless by now.

When they eventually emerged from the shop with their various packages they were giggling like a couple of naughty schoolgirls.

'I've never spent so much on myself in the whole of my life!' laughed Charlotte.

'Well, you deserve it,' said Jane, feeling pleased that it had been such a success. 'You'll look stunning tonight.' She paused and chose her words carefully. 'You know, I can't help thinking you'd look fantastic if your hair was cut to shoulder-length. It would still be long, but you'd be able to wear it down as well as up in a chignon.'

'I must admit I'm getting a bit fed up with the weight of it, tucked away in my nursing cap . . .'

'I'll take you to my hairdresser. He'll fit you in if he possibly can.' Strike while the iron's hot! thought Jane gleefully.

Charlotte gazed in the mirror as the hairdresser finished blowdrying the new, shorter length. Her hair shone under the bright fluorescent lights,

framing her face with a softer alluring look. She
barely recognised herself!

'It's perfect!' Jane stood up and came across
the crowded salon. 'Thanks, Henri; you've done
wonders!'

The small Chinese patron preened himself,
knowing that it was true. He had given the
young lady a completely new image. When she
had first walked in, she had seemed shy and
gauche, but look at her now, wreathed in smiles!
He accepted the generous tip from young Mrs
Frobisher, placed discreetly in the pocket of his
jacket, and escorted the two ladies to the door.

'Are you going out somewhere special tonight?'
he asked deferentially, as he held open the door.

'Just a quiet dinner party at home, Henri—
which reminds me, we'd better get a move on,
I've got a million things to do before Mark gets
back from the hospital . . .'

Jane drove up the Peak road like a taxi-driver,
taking the hairpin bends with an expertise born
of practice and desperation.

Wai Yee met them at the door, carrying
Samantha on her hip. She looked anxiously at
her mistress. There was so much to be done,
and she couldn't get down to it if she had to
amuse the little one. She was usually such a
good baby, but this afternoon . . .! It was as if
she sensed there was going to be a big occasion
and she wanted to be part of it.

As if reading the maid's thoughts, Jane reached
for her daughter and said briskly, 'Would you
look after Samantha until it's time for her feed,
Charlotte? I'd better help Wai Yee in the
kitchen.'

'I'd love to.' Charlotte took the cuddly baby

in her arms and was rewarded with a cherubic smile.

'Take her up to the nursery. There are lots of toys up there . . .' Jane was hurrying in to the house, her mind intent on the evening's menu.

Alone in the nursery with her precious charge, Charlotte walked out on to the balcony. 'Look at the ships out there on the sea, Samantha. Isn't that a wonderful sight?' She found herself peering into the distance towards Cheung Lau. Adam would be too involved with the refugees to break away for a dinner party. She was sure of it. What a pity! She would have liked him to see her in the new dress and hairdo.

She raised a cautious hand to her hair. What would he think of it when she did see him? Would he approve? Probably wouldn't even notice. Tucked away under her cap, it wouldn't show, and it was unlikely he would ever take her out again.

She put the baby down on her play mat and jingled one of her musical toys above her. Must stop thinking about him! she scolded herself. He's becoming an obsession, and it's all so futile!

'Who's a pretty little girl, then!' She smiled down at Samantha, who gurgled with delight at having this nice new lady all to herself.

It seemed a long time before Jane came to relieve her in the nursery. Samantha was demanding more and more attention, and it wasn't as if she could give her a feeding bottle to help out.

'Sorry I've been so long, but they're all panicking down there. It's not a difficult menu, but my cook is such a perfectionist. And then Mark arrived . . . Go and relax for a bit in your room. There's plenty of time before the others arrive.'

The luxurious guest suite was cool and inviting. The only sound was the gentle hum of the air-conditioning, as Charlotte trod gently over the thick pile carpet. It was designed for dual occupancy. Charlotte looked at the huge king-size bed with its expensive silk quilt, thinking how small she would feel in it tonight, all by herself. She went through into the elegant bathroom and peeled off her clothes. A hot bath, that was what she needed.

She lay in the scented water, revelling in the aura of luxury. Why hadn't she asked Jane who was coming to the dinner party? she wondered. It would have put her out of her misery. Anyway, she would dress herself as if she expected Adam to come, and then if, by some miracle he had been invited, and had accepted, and had made the journey across the water . . .

Oh, it's all too unlikely! she told herself crossly, stepping out on to the soft bath mat and reaching for a large fluffy towel.

She took her time getting dressed, however. No point in rushing things. The new dress fitted her like a dream. She twirled round in front of the mirror like a teenager going to her first school dance. From downstairs came the murmur of voices. The guests were beginning to arrive.

She started off down the staircase, and there he was! But he wasn't alone. His attractive auburn-haired companion was chatting vivaciously with Jane.

'Ah, there you are, Charlotte.' Her friend broke off to smile approvingly. 'This is Jenny Benson— Helen's sister. She's over here on holiday from Australia. And of course, you work with Adam, so there's no introduction needed there . . .'

Charlotte's heart was turning somersaults! He looked even more fabulous than usual. He was wearing the white tuxedo—*her* tuxedo, she liked to think of it!—and he was staring at her as if she were a ghost.

'Charlotte . . . I wouldn't have recognised you,' he said unsteadily. What a transformation! he was thinking.

'Doesn't she look marvellous this evening?' Mark Frobisher had joined his wife in welcoming the guests and he put out a hand to touch Charlotte's hair. 'What do you think of the new hairstyle, Adam? Rather stunning, don't you think?'

'I'm glad you didn't have it all cut off,' was his quiet reply. 'I like long hair.' He smiled down at her, his deep blue eyes sending shivers down her spine.

'Come into the drawing room and meet the others.' Jane was sweeping everyone along with her.

They were all of the medical fraternity. Charlotte was introduced to so many doctors and Sisters from St Margaret's that she promptly forgot all their names. There was no one from Cheung Lau except herself—and Adam.

Perhaps that was why Jane put them next to each other at dinner, she thought logically, as she toyed with her chopsticks, feeling terribly conscious of that strong masculine presence beside her. If she moved her leg even a fraction of an inch she would be able to touch him . . .

'So how's the weekend going? I must say you look as if you've been away on holiday.' He couldn't keep the admiration from his voice, however he tried. Was this really the timid little mouse who had plagued and embarrassed him when she first came to Hong Kong?

'It's going very well. We went shopping this afternoon . . .'

'So I see!' His eyes swept over her figure, noting the cinched-in waistline, the soft curve of her breasts beneath the filmy gown. He drew in his breath. It was all too much! She was having a disastrous effect on him. He mustn't become involved . . .

'I didn't expect to see you here tonight.' She raised her innocent blue eyes to his.

'Charles Gordon came over for the afternoon and offered to stay on,' Adam explained. 'He thought I needed a break. Come to think of it, I haven't been off the island for ages.'

'How was Wing Tai when you left? I thought he . . .'

'Don't talk shop, you two!' Jenny Benson leaned across from the other side of Adam and wagged a perfectly manicured finger. 'It's not fair on us non-medics.'

'Which non-medics?' asked Adam, and they all laughed.

'Well, me for a start,' Jenny replied, a trifle testily. 'I do like to understand the conversation. I always tell Helen to shut up if she goes on about the hospital.'

Charlotte glanced at the well-groomed Australian, thinking that she didn't look a bit like her sister. She was definitely older—possibly mid-thirties? It was difficult to guess under all that make-up. Obviously not in the medical profession. I wonder what she does . . . she thought.

'Have you seen Jenny on the box?' asked Adam, as if reading her thoughts.

She looked puzzled. 'You mean . . .'

'They don't get my programme over here, Adam,' Jenny interrupted quickly. 'You should know that. I mean, you've never seen me, have you?'

'No, but then I never watch television.'

'Jenny hosts a chat show in Australia,' supplied Jane, coming to the rescue, like the perfect hostess.

'I see.' That would account for the rather artificial make-up, Charlotte thought. She looks as if she lives permanently under a spotlight. 'Are you enjoying your holiday?' she asked politely.

'Oh, very much.' The Australian drawl was more pronounced than that of her sister. 'I think Hong Kong is *the* most exciting city in the world. And now I'm going to come out to see your little island of Cheung Lau. Adam has promised to show me all the beauty spots. It sounds very picturesque.'

The surgeon was smiling at Jenny, taking in every word she said.

I notice he hasn't picked her up on the word 'picturesque' as he did with me! Charlotte thought bitterly, recognising with dismay that her feelings were akin to jealousy. Cool it, girl! He has a right to entertain who he pleases . . .

'I understand the swimming is particularly good,' observed Jenny.

Charlotte nodded. Somehow she couldn't imagine the impeccable television celebrity jumping into the sea from one of the deserted beaches. She glanced at Adam, remembering him as he ran down the warm sand in his tight black swimming trunks.

He turned at the very same moment, and their

eyes met in a long, lingering, highly satisfying look. She wondered what he was thinking. Did he like what he saw? There was something in his manner that hadn't been there before.

The servants were clearing away some of the dishes. As always, at a Chinese dinner, there seems to be almost as much at the end as the beginning, Jane was thinking. She watched the plates of crab shells, duckling bones and mounds of rice disappear into the kitchen, wondering if they could cope without her. There was only the coffee to be served now, and Mark would produce some of his excellent brandy . . .

She glanced down the length of the table to her husband. He had been watching her as her mind ticked over. Unseen by the chattering guests, he blew her a kiss and she pursed her lips as if to catch it. Oh, she was so happy! It was wonderful to be so much in love. I wish Charlotte could find someone, she was thinking. Someone like Adam, perhaps?

Their heads were close together and they seemed deep in conversation. Jane smiled to herself. Stranger things had happened before.

The party moved into the drawing room in a haze of blue cigar smoke. There was a relaxed atmosphere as the guests sank into the comfortable armchairs. In spite of the attempt to avoid talking shop, the conversation veered inevitably to medical matters.

'Such an interesting case. I said to Charles . . .' 'And you should have seen the size of it!' 'Incredible! Never in the whole of my career . . .'

Charlotte crept out on to the balcony. The only non-medical discussion seemed to be taking place between Adam and Jenny, who were talking animatedly in a corner of the room, to the exclusion of all around them. She looked out across the twinkling lights of Hong Kong to the dark, mysterious sea beyond. The brilliant illuminations of the Star Ferry lit up the water as it ploughed its way over to Kowloon, laden with returning merrymakers, looking forward to their Sunday lie-in. Overhead, a large crescent moon winked down at her. The tall skyscrapers shone their neon signs over the city, standing tall and proud amid the hurly-burly of the Saturday crowds.

Suddenly she felt small and lonely and frightened—frightened of the future and what it might hold for her. She had known such happiness during the last few weeks. If only it could go on and on and . . .

A slight sound on the balcony made her turn towards the long casement windows. She could make out a tall, masculine figure coming towards her in the half light.

'Why so sad?' Adam's voice was gentle as he stared down at her.

A shadow obscured his eyes. She couldn't see the expression in them. Why had he come out and left his amusing companion? 'I'm not sad,' she began, her voice trembling at the nearness of him. 'Confused perhaps, but . . .'

'Confused?' She could hear the concern he felt for her and her pulses raced. He reached out and cupped a hand under her chin. 'Why are you confused, little one?'

He was standing so close that she could feel the beating of his heart. Could he feel hers? she wondered. Would he suddenly tell her that he knew her secret, that he had diagnosed what was wrong with her, and he was going to operate and

put everything right? And then when she was
healthy again, he was going to carry her off . . .

'Why, you're crying!' He reached into his breast
pocket and wiped a tear from her face with his
large white handkerchief. 'I wish you'd tell me
what's wrong.'

He bent his lips to her cheek and kissed the
salty skin where the tear had fallen. She tensed as
a wave of emotion swept over her.

'Oh, Charlotte . . .' His lips sought hers and
she melted against him, her body moulding against
his as naturally as if they were lovers. She felt the
strong contours of his manly frame pulsating
against her in a wild arousal.

A soft moan escaped her lips as his kiss strayed
down her soft neck and across her bare shoulders.
A warm sensation of desire flooded through her
body as she abandoned herself to his caresses. She
had never experienced anything like the feelings
that had claimed her. Yes, this was love . . . this
was the man she loved. This was her destiny . . .
to love and be loved . . .

'Adam, is that you?'

How long they had been locked together in
their tender embrace, Charlotte didn't know—nor
did she care. Time had ceased to exist; but the
sound of that strident Australian voice brought
them both back to earth.

Adam stepped back, his strong arms falling
reluctantly to his sides. 'Yes, I'm over here,
Jenny.' There was no disguising the frustration in
his voice.

'I say, what a beautiful view! Almost as good as
Sydney Harbour.' She laughed at her little joke,
and Adam smiled politely, a wave of anxiety
suddenly flooding through him. How on earth

could he have allowed himself to get carried away like that? What must the poor girl think of him? But she looked so beautiful, standing there in the moonlight like someone out of a fairy-tale. Yes, she'd looked like Cinderella at the ball.

He smiled at his romantic notions. He wasn't usually like this. The girl had bewitched him! The Australian had wandered across to the other end of the balcony. He leaned forward and brushed his lips against Charlotte's cheek.

'I'm sorry, Cinderella,' he whispered. 'I think your carriage has just arrived. Better go in before it turns into a pumpkin!

What on earth was he talking about? Charlotte watched as he joined Jenny by the railing. He must be going mad! He must have taken leave of his senses . . .'

She rubbed the warm, moist spot where he had kissed her and a feeling of unreality took over as she went back into the brightly lit room.

As she lay in the huge bed, after all the guests had gone, she even doubted whether it had all happened as she remembered it. Had that really been Adam out there on the balcony? Or had it been a figment of her imagination—something she had wished for so much that it had actually happened . . .

CHAPTER SEVEN

By the end of the next week, all the refugees had gone. A fleet of police launches had ferried them across to Kowloon and the army camps in the New Territories. Charlotte couldn't bear to watch them go. She threw herself into her work with a new vigour so that she had no time to worry about her departing patients. Perhaps she could go over and see them when they had settled in. She determined to ask Adam, but she would have to choose the right moment. He had been very cool and distant with her since last weekend.

Not surprising! she thought with a sigh. He must be cursing himself! Whatever had got into him? It must have been the wine, or the sudden freedom from duty after a heavy schedule. She could think of any number of reasons why the surgeon might have reacted as he did, but love was not one of them. No, it had been a mild, momentary flirtation, which he now regretted.

She was back on the medical ward with Sister Chen breathing down her neck at every move. They had admitted several new chest cases over the last few days. Something has got to be done about the acceptance of smoking as a way of life, Charlotte thought as she listened to Mr Chang's chest. She could hear the dreadful

deadly fluid ensconced in his lungs, and there
was no way she could eliminate it. He was forty-
five years old, and a lifetime of chain-smoking
had produced the onset of broncho-pneumonia,
for which he had been admitted.

'You're over the worst, Mr Chang. We
shouldn't need the oxygen tent again.' She
pushed back the apparatus from the bed. Better
not take it away, though. Just in case . . .

The small yellow-skinned man wheezed his
thanks. 'I go home soon?' he asked eagerly.
However were his family going to manage
without him? He hadn't caught any fish for two
weeks now. My brother will be looking after
them, he was thinking, but he cannot feed two
families for any length of time . . .

'As soon as Dr Forster agrees that you are
well enough, but it won't be for some time.'

He frowned, feeling the old, familiar craving
coming back, now that he could breathe unaided.
'I need cigarette,' he announced in a quiet,
matter-of-fact voice.

Charlotte couldn't believe her ears. It was all
she could do to prevent herself from shaking the
patient. 'You can't have a cigarette. Cigarettes
are bad for your chest. That's why you became
ill in the first place. Surely you must realise . . .'

'I don't think this is the time to lecture Mr
Chang, Nurse.' Sister Chen had swept across
from her desk. Sometimes this girl went beyond
the bounds of her responsibility! she thought
crossly. 'It's the doctor's place to explain the
treatment of a patient . . .'

'This isn't treatment, Sister, it's plain common
sense! Nobody but a complete idiot would
continue to smoke with a chest like that!'

'That's enough, Nurse Craven. Leave the matter to Dr Forster or . . .'

'What's the problem, ladies?' Adam was swinging easily down the ward, alarmed at the raised voices. Those two just couldn't hit it off! A definite clash of personalities, he diagnosed.

'Oh, Dr Forster, I'm glad you're here.' Sister Chen smiled ingratiatingly. 'Perhaps you will put Nurse Craven in her place,' she whispered, so that the patient couldn't hear.

Adam looked at the irate nurse. He had heard every word, from the other side of the ward, and he fully supported Charlotte in her no smoking campaign. He felt ashamed even of his occasional cigar after dinner, but they were few and far between and definitely for special occasions. But he would have to be diplomatic because Sister Chen was spoiling for a fight.

'I think it's a good idea to explain about the dangers of smoking, while the patient is actually in the hospital environment . . . on the other hand,' he added hastily, as he saw the thunderous look on the older woman's face, 'we have to choose our moment carefully, so it's probably better if I do the talking.'

Sister Chen smiled complacently and moved back to her desk. Adam's face was solemn, but as soon as they were alone he gave her a slow wink over the top of the patient's head, and she smiled with relief. He could be so understanding!

'I'm sure you have other duties to attend to, Nurse,' he said, in a staged voice.

'Yes, of course, sir.' She moved on to the next bed, revelling in the rosy glow that suffused her whenever Adam came near.

'When you've finished the TPRs and blood

pressures, Nurse Craven, I'd like you to give Mrs Wu a bath,' said Sister Chen.

'A proper bath, Sister?'

'Of course a proper bath, what other kind is there?'

There's a straightforward bed-bath for a start! Charlotte bit back her reply. Mrs Wu had only just started taking a bath in the bathroom. Her crippling deformities made it extremely difficult, but the grateful smile on her face as she was lowered into the soothing water made it all worth while. 'I shall need some help,' she said. 'Mrs Wu may be small, but she's no lightweight.'

'Of course you will,' said Sister smoothly. 'I wouldn't dream of taxing your strength. Nurse Lee will be free to help you soon.'

Suzie Lee smiled sympathetically as they lowered Mrs Wu into the bath. 'Cheer up, Charlotte! You won't be on Medical much longer.'

'I won't be out here much longer, and I'd like to get away from Sister Chen for my last few weeks.'

Mrs Wu pricked up her ears and smiled all over her olive-skinned, round, dimply face. She had understood the last sentence and could appreciate the young nurse's dilemma. Sister Chen was not her favourite person, either. A good efficient Sister—there was no doubt about that—but a real tartar, especially where the nurses were concerned. She gripped Nurse Craven's hand tightly, partly out of sympathy, but mainly because she was afraid that if the nurse relaxed her grip, she would float under the surface of the warm, soapy water. It felt so wonderful to be free of the restricting clothes

that exacerbated her pain. She closed her eyes,
wishing she could stay in the water all day. The
nurses chatted happily above her, and she
listened in occasionally when she heard a few
words she could understand. If I keep very still,
they might let me stay in a long time, she was
thinking . . .

'I think Mrs Wu has had long enough, now.'
Sister poked her head round the door. 'There's
work to be done on the ward, when you've
finished.'

The door swung to. 'The old bag!' murmured
Suzie Lee, and Charlotte laughed. It seemed
strange to hear her Chinese friend talking like
that.

'You forget, I trained in London too,' Suzie
said chirpily, then wished she hadn't. Training
was something you didn't talk about when
Charlotte was around. She was an expert nurse,
but on paper she was still unqualified. I wonder
when she'll get around to it, she was thinking.
Perhaps when she goes back to the UK?

'Come on, Mrs Wu. Put your arms round my
neck, and hold tight . . . that's the way!'
Charlotte was hauling the patient out of the
bath, and Suzie leaned across to envelop her in
a large towel.

'Velly good.' The patient smiled her thanks as
they smoothed down the counterpane at the end
of the proceedings. She felt so much better.

'Have you got everything you need?' asked
Charlotte, and Suzie repeated the question in
Cantonese. It was important that the rheumatoid
arthritis patient had everything to hand. If she
tried to lean over to her locker she might easily
fall out of bed.

Mrs Wu nodded. 'Thank you. Thank you yelly much.'

At the end of the day, Charlotte was feeling more tired than usual. It was all she could do to summon up the strength to go into the dining room for supper. And she usually looked forward to her meals here. Still, it had been a long hard week, and losing the refugees had been emotionally draining. She remembered the look of triumph on Sergeant Leung's face as they had straggled down to the waiting police launches. She had hung out of the hospital window, hoping to catch a last glimpse of Wing Tai and Yin Fen, but she couldn't make out their small figures amid all the confusion. Adam had supervised the whole manoeuvre, a grim, resigned expression on his face.

The dining room was almost full. 'Charlotte, over here!' called a voice.

She looked across to see who had called her name and was surprised to see the exquisitely dressed Jenny Benson. She had obviously made some attempt to appear casual, but the designer catsuit was superbly cut and the swathes of expensive gold chains around her neck looked incongruous. Charlotte felt grubby and very end-of-the-day. She wished she'd gone straight to her room for a shower and skipped supper.

'Why, Jenny, what a nice surprise! What brings you here?' She sank down on the chair next to the vivacious-looking Australian.

'I told you I was coming out to see your little island. Adam invited me . . . Talk of the devil!' Jenny beamed effusively as the tall, debonair figure approached their table.

'Have you been here long?' asked Adam.

He was obviously expecting her, thought Charlotte curiously, wondering what the attraction was. She wasn't what she would have considered to be Adam's type—whatever that was! She was attractive in a well-groomed sort of way. She hesitated to define it as well-preserved—that would be too catty! But there was no denying that the svelte figure belonged to an older woman. Perhaps Adam went for the mature type—especially if they were successful in their career, as Jenny obviously was.

'I've only just got here. I missed the last ferry so I had to charter a boat,' she told him.

'I would have sent the hospital launch for you, but there's so much red tape nowadays. Anyway, you're here, which is the main thing. Has Mary taken your order?'

'Well, no. I didn't know what the procedure was. I thought I'd better wait for you, and then I saw your little nurse here . . .'

Charlotte wasn't sure she liked being described in such a patronising way, but she continued to smile politely throughout the meal. The other two carried on a continual conversation which virtually excluded her. The main topic of discussion was travel, and as she had never set foot out of Britain, before coming to Hong Kong, there was very little she could contribute. She listened to their tales of safaris in the desert, cruises in the Caribbean, and thought how nice it would be if she had time to go round the world before . . . before things became too difficult. She had lost her previous resignation. She wasn't going to give up without a struggle! As soon as she got back home, she was going to start her enquiries . . .

'You're very quiet, Charlotte.'

She smiled at the sudden concern of the surgeon. 'Perhaps that's because I've got nothing to say on the subject.'

'I'm sorry, I hope we're not boring you,' Jenny put in quickly. 'I thought everyone was interested in travel.'

'I enjoy listening; I find it fascinating, but as I've never really been anywhere I can't add any stories of my own.'

It sounded terribly naïve, even to her own ears. She watched Adam's reaction. He must be making an unfavourable comparison with the jet-setting celebrity.

Little did she know that he was thinking how much more confident Charlotte was now. Difficult to believe this was the timid creature who couldn't say boo to a goose when she first arrived! She might not be able to contribute anything verbally, but just by being there she exuded an aura of intelligent interest. Lots of young women would have tried to get in on the conversation, for the sake of hearing their own voices. But dear little Charlotte sat bolt upright on her chair, drinking in their words, nodding and smiling occasionally and looking so incredibly beautiful—yes, beautiful! At last he'd admitted it to himself. He knew that beauty was in the eye of the beholder. He hadn't thought her beautiful when she first arrived—quite the reverse! And it wasn't simply that she'd had her hair styled and smartened herself up on the days he'd seen her in mufti. No, this was something indefinable . . . something that made his pulses race and his breath quicken . . . He was going to miss her when she returned to the UK at the end of the month. Perhaps it was as well she was going, before he made a fool of himself again . . .

'I've always wanted to travel. That was one of the reasons I came out here,' Charlotte continued quietly.

'And what was the other reason?' He couldn't resist the question, because, at the back of his mind, he wondered if her new-found confidence had anything to do with the broken love affair she had obviously suffered. Maybe she'd got over him at last—or perhaps she was going back to patch things up?

She smiled, a slow, sad smile that tore at his heart. 'You're not going to draw me so easily, Adam,' she said softly, and he felt the urge to take her in his arms again and smother her face with kisses. She's definitely a witch! he told himself sternly. Stop playing with fire!

'Well, whatever it was, I hope it's sorted itself out while you've been here,' he said aloud.

'Not entirely, but I'm feeling more positive now. I know what I have to do when I get home.'

She's so mysterious! It's infuriating! The sooner she goes, the better! Adam stood up from the table, scraping his chair noisily on the tiled floor in his effort to escape quickly.

'We can have coffee in my room, Jenny. And I've got a bottle of very good brandy . . .'

'Now you're talking!' Jenny shook her well-cut auburn hair and gave him a bright smile of approval. 'Oh, goodnight, Charlotte.' It was a polite afterthought. They seemed to have forgotten her.

'Yes, goodnight, Charlotte.' Adam turned briefly, to salve his conscience, and his heart went out to her; she looked so lonely as they left her.

But it's easier to nip it in the bud, he told himself unconvincingly.

Charlotte went to her room, taking her time so that she couldn't possibly run into them on the verandah. The windows were wide open to the cool evening air. It was only cool by comparison with the day; any breath of wind was welcome. She was glad they didn't have air-conditioning; it had made her throat dry at Jane's. Much nicer to breathe in the fresh air, straight from the sea.

She showered away the day's tension, trying hard not to think about the couple in the room not so very far from her own. It had nothing to do with her. Adam must know what he was doing with a sophisticated woman like that. Perhaps they had invited Sister Benson to join them? Somehow she doubted it . . . She towelled her hair vigorously and then lay back on the bed, the hair dryer at full blast. She didn't want to turn it off, in case she heard something she shouldn't!

When at last she was ready for bed, she stepped out on to the verandah for a last look at the moon. The soft sounds of the sea drifted up from the harbour, mingling with the gentle rustling of the breeze in the trees. There was laughter coming from the other end of the verandah. She recognised the loud, strident female voice. And then she could hear Adam, talking animatedly about something. The intensity of his deep tones drove a knife into her heart. She hurried inside quickly, shutting the windows firmly behind her.

Some time later she was awakened by the sound of horses' hooves. It was just like that last time—the night when Mai Ling had disappeared. She strained her ears to hear who was out there. The sound of Adam's voice was unmistakable, and he was not alone. Jenny Benson was still with him.

Charlotte got out of bed and crept over to the window, but the moon was hidden behind a cloud. She couldn't see a thing out there in the black night. But she could hear the departing horses and the voices of their riders.

Strange time for Adam to be showing Jenny round the island! she thought miserably, as she climbed back into bed and tried to go back to sleep.

When morning came, she felt like a wet rag. She had spent the night tossing and turning, worrying about Adam, wondering what he was up to and why he had taken Jenny with him on his mysterious mission.

But she needn't have worried about them because, when she went into the dining room for breakfast, they were seated at the same table, looking extremely pleased with themselves, and tucking into a hearty breakfast. Where had they spent the night? It's none of your business, she told herself sternly, as she put on her social smile and sat down beside Jenny.

'My, you're up early!' She couldn't resist an attempt to embarrass them, but it was water off a duck's back.

Jenny laughed and smiled conspiratorially at Adam. 'Yes, aren't we? Well, it's the early bird that catches the worm, you know. This scrambled egg is delicious—I'm glad your cook can do cooked breakfast, because I'm starving. How about you, Adam?'

He nodded, carefully avoiding Charlotte's eyes. What must she be thinking of him? He wished

Jenny wouldn't make it so obvious that they'd been together all night.

'You look tired, Charlotte,' he said, suffering a pang of conscience at the sight of her drawn face.

'I didn't sleep well last night.'

Had she heard them going off? he wondered. He stared into her eyes enquiringly, but she was giving nothing away. They would have to be more careful. It was obvious she suspected something.

Helen Benson breezed into the dining room, looking bright and efficient in her crisp blue Sister's uniform.

'Jenny, I didn't know you were still here! Someone said they'd seen you last night. How are you?'

'Fine. Come and have some of this scrambled egg . . .'

'No, thanks. Just coffee for me.' Helen sat down beside her sister. 'I've got to watch my figure. Not like you.'

'Oh, I'll go on a crash diet when I go back home,' laughed Jenny. 'And I do a work-out every day at the gym. Got to do in my business. If I'm three pounds overweight it shows on the small screen. How do you stay so slim, Charlotte?'

'She's not slim, she's skinny,' Adam put in, then noticed the hurt look in her eyes. Did she really care about what he thought?

'I've never had a weight problem,' Charlotte said quietly. 'Quite the reverse.'

'Well, you're lucky . . .' The two sisters were chattering along about the problems of dieting and getting clothes to fit them. Charlotte had ceased to listen. She ate her breakfast hastily, and left them to it.

Adam too excused himself. The idle female

gossip was not his scene. 'Just a minute, Charlotte.'
He caught up with the trim little figure in her
becoming white uniform. 'What's the rush?'

'Sister Chen likes her nurses to get in on time,'
she replied, with a mischievous grin.

'I'm sure she does, but you're ridiculously early
today. If I didn't know you better, I'd say you
were trying to get away from people.'

She turned her innocent blue eyes on him.
'Whatever gave you that idea?'

He laughed boyishly, and her heart turned over.
'Actually, I was going to ask Sister if I could
borrow you for the morning to help me in
Outpatients,' Adam told her. 'I've got a long list
of appointments plus the inevitable patients who
simply turn up expecting to be seen.'

She hesitated, knowing that she had no choice
in the matter. He was the boss. She was surprised
he had even broached the subject before speaking
to Sister. Usually she was simply told where she
was supposed to work.

'I should find that very interesting,' she said
cautiously.

'Good. I'll see you in about half an hour, then.'
He strode off to tackle Sister Chen, wondering
why he had invented the excuse of being busy. He
would have to move one of the juniors to Surgical
for the morning . . .

CHAPTER EIGHT

It seemed strangely quiet in Outpatients. Charlotte busied herself checking trays and trolleys, putting clean sheets on the examination couches and generally making herself useful. Sister Benson smiled her approval at her nurse, but couldn't help thinking it was strange of Adam to have asked for her to be moved here. It wasn't as if they had many appointments that morning. Still, there were sure to be some casual patients who simply dropped in for advice or a bottle of cough medicine to soothe their nicotine-polluted chests. It couldn't be that he'd taken a shine to Nurse Craven, could it? No, Adam was far too professional for that. He might have played around a bit—and rumour had it that he'd broken a few hearts in various corners of the world!—but he never allowed his private life to encroach on his professional activities. Besides, the girl was too quiet and serious for the flamboyant surgeon. Jenny was more his type . . .

'What would you like me to do next, Sister?' asked Charlotte.

Good question! 'Perhaps you'd like to see if Dr Forster is ready for you, Nurse.' Pass the buck! She was his responsibility, after all.

Adam was reading through his case notes and looked up irritably when Charlotte went into his consulting room. 'The first patient hasn't arrived yet. I'll ring when I need you—unless you'd like to read up some of this morning's cases.' He'd requested her transfer; the least he could do was give the poor girl some instruction.

'Thanks. I'd like that.' Always useful to know the patient's background. She perched on the edge of a chair at the other side of the great man's desk and leafed through the pile of notes.

'I see we have a lot of ante-natal patients,' she remarked quietly.

'Yes, we've made quite a break-through in that direction. There was considerable opposition at first. Chinese women are traditionally opposed to any idea of lying in, but when they found that we were happy to discharge them on the same day, if there were no complications, they came flocking to us. They enjoy the ante-natal care we give them and they keep coming back afterwards to see us. Sometimes it's more like a social club, with the women who've just dropped in for a gossip, but at least we can keep tabs on them. Do you like obstetrics?'

'Yes; I found it totally absorbing when I worked in the surgery with my father. Of course, I'll have to get my SRN before I can go on to do midwifery . . .'

'So you are considering it, then?'

Was she? She hadn't thought about what she was saying. It had been her dearest wish, all the time she was nursing her mother, but now things were different, weren't they? And she had actually forgotten her precarious health problem. Well, that was a step in the right direction! She smiled broadly, and Adam caught a glimpse of even, pearly white teeth. 'Yes, I'm considering it.' Well, she could dream, couldn't she? No harm in that . . .

'I think you should.' He sounded deeply concerned.

She nodded. 'I'll go and see if the first patient is here yet.' She escaped quickly, not wanting to get into a difficult discussion about her future.

The first patient had brought the whole family with her—mother, aunt, and two small sons. The children squatted on the floor beneath their mother's bulge and the older women watched the official-looking nurse in the white dress coming towards them. They hadn't seen this one before. It was to be hoped she knew what she was doing. She looked very young and couldn't possibly have babies of her own, and if you've never had your own baby, how can you possibly advise anyone else? I don't hold with all this new-fangled medicine, the old aunt was thinking.

'Mrs Pang?' asked Charlotte hopefully.

The young mother nodded wearily. Let's get this over with, she was thinking. I've got a million things to do besides waste my time in this strange-smelling hospital. But I promised that nice doctor I would return . . .

'Would you like to come this way, please?'

The older women started to get up too, but Charlotte assured them they would be more use looking after the two little boys, who were already restless.

The old aunt sniffed disapprovingly. Bossy young thing! she thought. I told my sister it was all a big mistake letting her daughter come to one of these places. Six sons I have, not to mention the daughters, and never needed a doctor. The world's gone soft! I used to work all morning in the fields, have one of the babies in the afternoon, and I was still expected to cook the evening meal. She shook her head uncomprehendingly, as she watched her niece waddling towards the doctor's room, helped along by the skinny young English nurse, for all the world as if she were some kind of invalid!

'Mrs Pang, how nice to see you again,' Adam said, and he really meant it. He had grave doubts about whether this patient would return for her full ante-natal care. And it wasn't going to be an easy confinement, especially if the foetus had reverted to its breech position. He launched into fluent Cantonese, making quick notes of her answers to his questions. No, she wasn't feeling too well—not as well as she'd felt with the others. Yes, it was uncomfortable most of the time, but then she hadn't long to go. She could tell it was almost due, and her aunt, who knew all about these things, had told her . . .

'Quite! Well, let's have a look, shall we? Nurse Craven, if you wouldn't mind, we'll get her up on the couch . . . good. Now just relax.'

Charlotte watched his face as he palpated the abdomen and could tell that something was wrong. 'I'm going to have to admit her,' he whispered. 'The foetus has turned back again and it's quite definitely a breech presentation. If I let her go, we may not see her back here again, and I don't fancy her chances if she has a home delivery.'

Mrs Pang looked anxiously at the doctor. It was a good thing he spoke her language. 'Is everything all right, Doctor?' she asked tentatively.

No good being evasive, but he didn't want to

frighten her. 'The baby's fine—feels strong and sturdy . . .'

'It's a boy,' she announced proudly.

Adam smiled. 'You think so?'

'I know so.' She started to raise herself from the couch.

'There's just one problem.' He tried to explain about the position of the baby, but she frowned, unwilling to accept that there was anything wrong. She had borne two sons before, without any difficulty. Why should this one be any different?

'I'm going to admit you, so that we can keep an eye on you, and when the time comes for your delivery . . .'

'No! I have to go back to my family.'

Adam pulled the cotton sheet over the patient's abdomen. 'Nurse Craven, would you ask Mrs Pang's mother to come in for a moment.'

He hadn't bargained for the appearance of both the older women, but they were inseparable. Lai Ming Pang's mother had been dominated by her older sister for the whole of her life and she couldn't possibly cope without her. They shuffled into the doctor's room, glancing round uncertainly at the weird instruments and dressings. It looked more like a torture chamber than a place where you had babies!

Adam took a deep breath and tried to explain what he intended to do. As soon as they grasped his meaning, all three women started to cry. From outside the door came the sound of loud wailing from the little boys, who were feeling neglected, and detected that all was not well.

'Go and see to those children, while I cope

with this little problem,' he said to Charlotte,
with a wry grin.

She gave him a sympathetic smile as she closed
the door on her way out. He was going to need
all his considerable powers of persuasion!

Later that morning, she had to admit that he
was adept at getting his own way. How he did
it, she didn't know, but after a few minutes he
always managed to get the patients eating out of
his hand! She wondered what his secret was.
Probably just sheer charm, and a magnetic
personality. Anyway, whatever it was, it had
worked on the Pang family. The young mother
was ensconced in Obstetrics enjoying her unexpected leisure, and the senior members had gone
away smiling and nodding their approval of the
clever young doctor. He seemed to know what
he was talking about, the old aunt had admitted
grudgingly, and he had taken the trouble to
learn their language, so he must be a decent
sort.

The morning passed quickly. Charlotte felt
almost sad when it was time to go for lunch.
Adam looked up briefly when she told him Sister
Benson was sending her to first sitting.

'Thanks for your help, Nurse,' he said.

'I'm officially off duty this afternoon, but if
you need me here, I could . . .'

'No, that's OK; I'm nearly through. You go
off and enjoy yourself. You're back on Medical
this evening.'

She smiled. 'I bet Sister Chen's missed me,'
she said softly, and he gave her a sympathetic
smile before bending back over his patient.

She walked down the corridor to the dining
room, feeling strangely deflated. It had been

such fun working with Adam. She loved the aura of authority he exuded, coupled with his gentle bedside manner. And there was something about the way he placed his long sensitive fingers with the fine blond hairs on to the patients' skin that was so disturbing to her. She liked the way his eyes took on a caring look as he listened to a patient recounting a problem. Oh, he was a wonderful doctor! He was a wonderful man!

'You look pleased with yourself,' remarked Suzie Lee, as Charlotte sat down beside her. 'Did you enjoy your morning in Outpatients?'

Charlotte came down to earth quickly. 'Yes, it was very interesting.'

'I was in Obstetrics when we admitted your breech case. The old dears with her were saying all sorts of nice things about Dr Forster. They seemed to have forgotten that I speak the lingo. I think they quite fancied him!'

Charlotte smiled to herself. That wasn't difficult! 'Are you off duty this afternoon, Suzie?' she asked.

'No, I'm not free till this evening.'

'Pity; I was going to suggest we went swimming together. I feel like getting away from hospital.'

'Another time.'

Charlotte nodded, wondering what she was going to do with herself. She usually enjoyed her own company, but for once in her life, she didn't want to be alone. She felt restless. Well, there was nothing to stop her going off for a swim by herself. She'd done it once before.

Strange, she'd never wanted to repeat the experience, although the sight of Adam diving into the water had continued to haunt her ever since. She put down her chopsticks. Mary's fried chicken and mushrooms was delicious, as always, but she'd lost her appetite.

Back in her little room, she moved quickly before she could change her mind. The walk over the hill would do her good and she could swim and return to hospital with plenty of time to spare. She stuffed her bikini into her shoulder-bag and set off up the little path.

The hot afternoon sun beat down on her back. She was glad she'd remembered to wear a cotton shirt with long sleeves because the sun's rays could be harmful at this time of the year. It will be great to cool off in the sea, she was thinking as she rounded the summit of the hill and looked down at the bay on the other side of the island.

She caught her breath in amazement. There, below her on the shore, was a group of children laughing and shouting, plunging in and out of the waves with gay abandon, just like any normal children. But these aren't normal children, she thought, with a shiver of apprehension. These are the children I saw last time, the children Adam had said didn't exist. And they had run away from her as if they were terrified of being seen.

She crouched down in the bushes and watched their antics. They seemed perfectly happy now. It would be a pity to spoil their fun. But wait a minute! Wasn't that . . .?

She gasped with surprise. There was no mistaking the plucky little boy hopping along the beach on his crutches. It was Wing Tai! Charlotte flung caution to the winds in her delight at seeing the young patient again, as she raced down the hill.

'Wing Tai! Wing Tai!' she cried exuberantly.

The children fell silent and stared at the unexpected apparition. Those in the water started for the shore. The oldest boy was already gathering the younger ones together, preparing for flight.

'No, wait! I'm not going to harm you.'

Wing Tai recognised his favourite nurse and grinned happily. 'She's OK,' he told the leader of the group quickly. 'We can trust her. Don't worry.'

The older boy frowned. He wasn't sure. He'd been told not to trust anyone, and he'd seen this woman snooping around the beach once before. He stood his ground, scowling in an unfriendly way as the intruder reached the sand.

Wing Tai took the initiative and moved forward on his crutches, with an expertise born of sheer determination.

'*Bonjour, madame. Je suis très content de vous revoir*,' he said, smiling his welcome.

'*Et moi aussi*. I'm thrilled to see you again. I thought you were over on Kowloon. Why are you still here, and who's looking after you?' Questions were pouring into Charlotte's mind as she hugged the little boy.

The group leader scowled and clutched at Wing Tai's sleeve. It was obvious that he wanted them to move off.

'*Vous venez avec nous*?' asked Wing Tai anxiously. He didn't want to lose the nice nurse now that they had met up again.

'I'd love to come with you,' Charlotte replied eagerly.

Wing Tai spoke rapidly to the older boy, who was by no means convinced, but eventually gave in grudgingly and set off along the beach.

All the children followed, their natural high spirits returning as they began to accept the newcomer. One little girl even sneaked up and put her hand in Charlotte's, when the leader wasn't looking. They came to a small stream running down from the hill across the sand. The child held up her small arms trustingly, for Charlotte to lift her over. When they reached the other side, she looked at Wing Tai, wondering how he would cope, but the resourceful young boy merely turned his crutches into an advantage and pole-vaulted across like an athlete.

'Bravo! What a boy!'

He beamed at her praise and turned back to watch the other children floundering across the water. At one point, he sat on the bank and held out a crutch for a small child to hold on to. Charlotte laughed. What a spirit the boy had!

They reached the end of the beach and started to climb up a path that led over a grassy knoll down into a quiet, densely wooded cove. If the children had not been with her, she would never have suspected it was there.

The path continued through thick green bushes, opening out on to a wide clearing, set back on to the hillside. The clearing was obviously new, but the building in the centre was extremely old. Charlotte stared in amazement at the beautiful temple. No one had told her there was a historic monument on the island. Surely this was worth a mention?

She followed Wing Tai down the path. He had no difficulty getting around except where the ground was uneven, and then he slowed his pace slightly. At first sight the temple appeared to be deserted. It rose up from the ornate terrace in wide stone tiers that reached up towards the tall trees on the hillside. Inside the air was cool and filled with the cloying odour of incense. The little girl was pulling her towards the altar, which was covered with oranges.

Perhaps it's their Harvest Festival, Charlotte thought, as she gazed down at the fruit. No, that's unlikely. There's no one out here except the children, and I don't suppose their customs are anything like ours. Probably just gifts placed on the altar. She reached out to touch the rich gold cloth. It was obvious that someone was taking great care of the temple.

'What do you think you're doing?'

She snatched back her hand as if she had been burned. 'Adam!' she exclaimed. He was the last person she had expected to see here.

His eyes were blazing with anger as he strode into the temple, his shoes echoing loudly on the ancient stone floor. The little girl dropped her hand quickly, and went back into the sunlight to join her friends. Even Wing Tai had deserted Charlotte. She found herself alone, in front of the awe-inspiring altar, staring up into the surgeon's furious face.

'How did you get here?' he thundered.

'The children brought me . . .'

'I told them they were never to . . .'

'It's not their fault. You mustn't be cross with them.' She stared beseechingly into his eyes.

His anger began to subside when he saw her look of fear. He had overreacted; but the children had been warned to keep out of sight. If they brought Charlotte here, they might just as easily bring . . .

'What's going on, Adam? I don't understand.'

Her plaintive voice touched at his heartstrings. Was it safe to tell her?

He took a step towards her and placed his hands on her shoulders. 'Let's go outside. This places gives me the creeps—too many spirits listening in!' He gave a hoarse laugh as he pulled her towards him. 'Poor Charlotte; I'm sorry if I frightened you.' He kissed the tip of her nose, and she could feel his hot breath on her face, before he turned away.

She followed him out into the sun, shielding her eyes against its savage rays. The children were nowhere to be seen.

'I hope the children are all right,' she said worriedly.

He smiled at her concern. 'They're in good hands. Come over here. It's cool in the courtyard, and we won't be distrubed.'

He took her hand gently in his own, and at the touch of his fingers she began to melt. Whatever he had to tell her, she didn't mind . . .

'Sit here.' He patted the antique stone bench, almost hidden from sight amid the broad leaves of the tropical plants. The air was filled with the busy droning of the insects on the hillside as she glanced up at his stern features with trepidation.

'You must keep secret everything I tell you now,' he began mysteriously. 'There would be grave consequences if the authorities were to raid my little hideaway . . .'

'But who are all these children . . .?'

'Hush, don't look so frightened! It's not as bad as you think. Yes, they are illegal refugees, but there's a purpose in my keeping them here. I'm involved in a desperate legal battle to set up a haven for refugees here on Cheung Lau. Hong

Kong reached saturation point some time age—hence the harsh measures. The colony had accepted more Vietnamese and Chinese refugees than any other country, but a halt had to be called to prevent overcrowding and too heavy a burden being placed on the social services . . .'

'So why are you fighting the authorities?'

'I'm not fighting the authorities!' he snapped. 'I'm going through the proper legal channels to allow my small settlement to be recognised. But it all takes time, and in the meantime I run up against red tape and arrogant little men like Sergeant Leung . . .' He broke off, running a hand through his hair with the characteristic gesture she had come to love.

'My poor Adam!' Charlotte reached forward and placed a hand on his forehead, wanting to soothe away the worried lines that had appeared.

He grasped her hand and brought it to his lips. 'You're such a comfort to me, Charlotte,' he murmured. 'I'm dreading the time when you have to leave me.' There, he'd voiced his thoughts out loud! At last she knew what he had been wanting to say for the past few weeks. This young, inexperienced woman had done what no other woman had ever done: she had made him fall in love. He was no longer in charge of his own destiny—and he loved the strange feeling that flooded through him.

'I need you. I want you with me all the time. Stay here in Hong Kong.' He pulled her roughly into his arms.

'Adam, I don't know what to say . . .'

His hungry mouth found hers in a long, passionate kiss. She closed her eyes and gave in to the ecstasy that was sweeping over her. It was all

so unreal. She felt his arms clinging to her body
as if they would never let go, and she responded
to his passion in a wild frenzy of pent-up emotion.
She had wanted him for so long, and now she was
like soft clay in the sculptor's hand . . .

They were lying on a soft rush mat at the edge of
the courtyard. Charlotte brushed a hand over her
cotton skirt and sat up, smiling down into the face
of the man she loved so much.

'Come here,' Adam whispered huskily, reaching
out his arms to pull her back to him.

'Shouldn't we go and find the children . . .'

His forceful lips silenced her again. 'Now we
can go,' he murmured, as he released her. 'I've
got a surprise for you.'

She loved the feel of his strong fingers as they
twined around hers, and the way his body swung
along rhythmically beside her. They crossed the
courtyard and went through a small garden.

'They even grow their own food now,' he told
her. 'We're becoming self-sufficient.'

She noted the pride in his voice as she looked
at the neat rows of vegetables. They went out
towards the hillside, where a series of wooden
huts, cleverly camouflaged by the trees, had been
built into the side of the hill. And there, outside
one of the shelters, a tiny girl was playing with a
doll. There was no mistaking her former patient!

'Yin Fen!' Charlotte exclaimed.

The girl was startled to hear her name. She
looked up and recognised her nurse at once.
Jumping to her feet, she ran across the beaten
earth and flung herself into Charlotte's arms.

Charlotte raised grateful eyes to Adam. 'Is this
my surprise?'

He nodded happily. 'I couldn't let her go with the others.'

'And Wing Tai as well. He's getting on well.'

'Yes, I ride over every day to see them. There's another ex-patient you'll recognise.' Adam led her into one of the huts, where a young girl was feeding her baby.

'Mai Ling! So this is where you brought her. But who looks after everybody?'

'The adults take care of the youngsters and we have a couple of Vietnamese nurses. But when I'm legally recognised . . .'

'So it's *when*, not *if*, I see?' Charlotte laughed.

'Of course. I always believe in being optimistic. For me there's no other way. I think if you refuse to accept defeat you usually get what you want.'

She listened to his forceful voice, wishing that she could be so positive. If only she had met Adam before!

'What's the matter, Charlotte?' He had noticed the worried look on her face.

'Nothing,' she answered quickly, wanting the dream to continue as long as possible. Soon she would wake herself up and face reality, but for the moment . . .

'Of course, my ultimate aim is to resettle all my refugees,' he went on. Perhaps if he told her more of his plans, she would forget whatever it was that was troubling her. He had come to recognise that faraway pensive look that told him all was not well. 'Jenny Benson is going to take Mai Ling and her baby back to Australia.'

A feeling of relief flooded through her. So that was the purpose of the clandestine journey in the night!

'I'm so glad—I mean . . .' She broke off sheepishly.

'I know what you mean,' he said laughingly. 'You thought I was having an affair with her, didn't you? Come on, admit it!'

'Well, the thought had crossed my mind.'

He seized her arms playfully, gazing down lovingly into her eyes. 'And were you jealous?' he asked softly.

'Yes, I was,' she admitted. 'Well, I would never have guessed she had a philanthropic streak.'

'She's a surprising lady. Beneath that brash exterior lurks a heart of gold. And she's got no children of her own and more money than she knows what to do with. Her husband . . .'

'I didn't know she was married.' More relief!

'She's been happily married for years, but the career always came first. Now that they want children, it's too late. We mustn't make the same mistake.'

Charlotte's heart missed a beat. Adam was staring down at her with an intensity she couldn't take. 'What are you saying, Adam?'

'I'm asking you to marry me,' he replied softly.

From somewhere in the background came the shrilling of a telephone. It seemed an incongruous sound out here in the middle of nowhere, but then Charlotte realised that Adam would have insisted on telephone communication between the hospital and his refugees. Her mind was deliberately refusing to register his question. It was all too improbable . . .

'Dr Forster, it's the hospital!' One of the Vietnamese nurses was waving through the window of the main hut.

'Saved by the bell,' he quipped, with a boyish grin. 'But don't go away. I'll be back.'

Charlotte remained rooted to the spot, her heart weeping inside her. All her being wanted to shout, 'Yes, oh yes, Adam Forster, I want to marry you'. But she couldn't condemn the man to a life with an invalid, even if she managed to survive the next year. He deserved a better life than she had enjoyed, watching her mother die . . .

His face was serious when he emerged from the hut. 'It's Mrs Pang—she's gone into labour. We'll have to get back. I may have to do a Caesar.'

The leader of the children had appeared with Adam's horse. He was relieved that the doctor wasn't mad at him for bringing the woman to the camp. Quite the reverse! He seemed very fond of her. He held the horse steady for the great man to mount, then helped the woman up behind him. She flashed him a grateful smile, although she looked scared stiff. He could tell she'd never been on a horse before! She'll be OK if she clings on to Dr Forster, he was thinking.

And that was exactly what she was doing. Her arms encircled his waist and she laid her head against his warm back and closed her eyes.

'Are you clinging tightly because you're frightened or because you love me?' he called over his shoulder.

'I'm petrified! Can you slow down a little?'

He laughed, as if he didn't have a care in the world. 'I'm sorry, little one, I didn't mean to scare you.' He reined in his horse at the top of the hill, and jumping down, lifted her out of the saddle. 'We must hurry, but I have to have your answer first.'

He was holding her very close. She looked up

into his tender eyes. The dying rays of the sun were casting a deep red glow over his blond hair as he stooped to kiss her, with parted lips.

When he released her, his eyes were full of expectancy.

'I can't give you an answer—not now. I have a problem . . . an insurmountable problem . . .'

'What sort of a problem?' He was frowning at her now.

'It . . . it's a medical problem,' she faltered.

Adam stared at her in amazement. 'Then we'll tackle it together—but later. We mustn't keep the patient waiting.' He was lifting her back on to the horse, talking all the while to keep up her flagging spirits. It couldn't possibly be anything serious, he was thinking. She must tell him all about it, later when they were alone . . .

They wound their way down the hillside back to the hospital, Adam keeping up his bright monologue. The sun had disappeared behind the hill and Charlotte's dream had gone with it. She was barely listening to his voice. He had no idea of what she was up against.

'I'll take you over to Hong Kong tomorrow to see the house I've bought. You're going to love it. We'll have the whole day to ourselves and you can tell me all about your little problem . . .'

'Dr Forster, thank goodness you're here!' Sister Benson came hurrying out of Reception at the sound of horses' hooves. Well, well, little Nurse Craven on the back! she registered. She averted her eyes as the doctor swung her easily down from the saddle. Sister Chen had already been along to complain that her less than favourite nurse had not yet returned from her afternoon off.

'How's Mrs Pang?' Adam asked breathlessly.

'She's in the delivery room . . .'

'I'm on my way.' He strode into the hospital, without a backward glance.

Charlotte hesitated. A feeling of unreality was sweeping over her. Could she possibly go back on duty as if nothing had happened?

'You'd better change as quickly as you can, Nurse,' Sister said gently, as she cast an experienced eye over the dishevelled girl. 'Sister Chen is champing at the bit.' She lowered her voice. 'But if I were you, I'd take it all with a pinch of salt. Her bark is much worse than her bite!'

Charlotte flashed her a grateful smile and hurried off to her little room. Minutes later she was on the ward, prepared for the worst.

'Ah, Nurse Craven, so you finally decided to return!'

Sister Chen's sarcasm was lost on her. This evening she didn't care what the old bag said to her. Adam Forster was in love with her, and that was all that mattered. He wanted to marry her. Until it was time to give him an answer, she could carry on with her hopeless dream . . .

'I don't think you've heard a word I've said, Nurse!'

'Sorry, Sister.' She was right about that!

'You'd better get on with your work. Nurse Lee is trying to cope with beds and backs all by herself.'

'Yes, Sister.' Charlotte moved away from the desk, as if she was on automatic pilot, a strange smile hovering on her lips.

The older woman shook her head in disbelief. The girl's taken leave of her senses! she thought. I'll have to speak to Sister Benson about her. We can't go on like this. When I was a nurse in training . . .

'What did she say to you?' hissed Suzie as Charlotte pushed her way through the curtains.

'I can't remember,' was her truthful reply. 'Hello, Mrs Wu. How are you this evening? Your back's looking much better.' Her professional interest returned as she looked down at the patient. Nursing was something she cared about, but the machinations of the powers that be left her cold. I suppose I'm rather like Adam in that respect, she mused as she straightened Mrs Wu's draw sheet. The very thought of him sent shivers down her spine. She wondered how he was getting on in the delivery room. She hoped nothing would go wrong with the birth; Mrs Pang was such a sweet patient.

Sister Chen kept her deliberately late that evening, but she didn't mind. Adam would be tied up in Obstetrics for hours. She paused outside the door as she went down the corridor, wanting to go inside and catch a glimpse of that damp fair head bending over his patient, but she thought better of it. Mustn't disturb his concentration . . .

She lay in her narrow bed watching the moon. It had been a long day. She would remember it for the rest of her life.

CHAPTER NINE

SISTER Chen was trembling with indignation when Charlotte arrived on duty next morning.

'Apparently I am to give you the day off. Dr Forster left some garbled message with the night nurse when he finished his Caesarian section . . .'

'Oh, he had to do a Caesar, then? Is the baby all right? Is it a boy or a girl?'

'I've no idea, Nurse. As I was saying, you may have the day off, but . . .'

'Would you like me to help with breakfasts, Sister?' Charlotte asked. 'I don't expect we'll be going off too early.'

'Yes, I would,' Sister conceded stiffly, wondering exactly what was going on between the surgeon and the little nurse. It seemed highly irregular. Well, she would have to make up the time later in the week.

Charlotte was clearing away the last plate when Adam came through the door. His hair was falling over his forehead and he looked tired and unshaven. Her heart went out to him.

'I thought I said Nurse Craven was to have the day off, Sister?' he snapped irritably.

'I've already said she can go, sir, but she volunteered to help with breakfasts.'

'Did she, indeed?' He moved across the ward. 'We're leaving in half an hour, Charlotte.'

Sister Chen pricked up her ears. She didn't approve of the use of first names on her ward. Not in front of the patients!

'How's Mrs Pang?' Charlotte gazed up into the deep blue eyes that she loved so much.

'She's well again. I did a Caesar under epidural and she was an excellent patient. Plucky little thing.'

'But what is it? she asked impatiently.

'Oh, it's a boy.' He smiled at her interest.

'She said it would be.'

'Yes, she's delighted about that. Three sons, and she's only twenty-one . . . Half an hour, I said. You'd better leave the ward now, and make yourself beautiful. Meet me in Reception.'

Charlotte's heart was fluttering as she watched the departing figure. She daren't look across at Sister! 'Meet me in Reception'—so they weren't simply going to sneak away. Adam had thrown caution to the winds. The whole hospital would know by lunchtime!

It was impossible to decide what to wear. He'd bought a house on Hong Kong. Would it be in the course of construction, or would it be fully completed? Should she look casual or smart—or what? In the end, she decided on her new cotton catsuit. She'd never worn one before as her parents had perferred her to wear a skirt or a dress, but Jane and the sales woman had assured her she looked terrific in it. And scarlet was just the colour to set off her fair hair—or so they had said! Charlotte rolled up her bikini and put it in her shoulder-bag. There just might be a pool at this house.

Most of the affluent people had one, and she didn't think Adam would have skimped on such a little extra . . .'

He was waiting for her when she walked into Reception, drumming his fingers impatiently on the desk. His eyes registered their approval of her appearance. It had been worth the extra effort.

'You look lovely,' he breathed softly.

She coloured deeply, as he took her hand and led her out through the main door. Sister Benson watched from the window. She had seen it coming, but she would never have thought it possible—Dr Forster and Nurse Craven—well, well! Whatever next?

They stepped into the launch and Jim, the boatman, set the engines in motion. He glanced at the eminent surgeon, sitting close to the pretty nurse. This didn't look like a professional trip to him. No, this was definitely pleasure!

The boat sped across the water towards Hong Kong Island. Charlotte looked shyly at Adam, noting that he had shaved since she had seen him on the ward, and his hair shone in the morning sunlight as if it was newly washed. She longed to run her fingers through it, but thought it would shock the young boatman, who kept glancing at them.

'I hope you'll like the house.' Adam turned to her with a smile. 'I bought it when I first came out—more as an investment than anything else—but now . . .'

'I'm sure I'll love it,' she said quickly. 'Where is it?'

'It's at Shek O, near the Frobisher beach house. I was very lucky to get it. Houses round there don't often come on the market, so Jane and Mark advised me to buy. It will be my first real home.'

She glanced at him curiously. 'But what about when you were a child?'

'I lived with my grandmother, and she preferred hotels to domesticity. My mother left my father and me when I was very small. She was involved with various charities and never had any time for me. She was always off travelling somewhere, and I got left behind. I suppose that's why I prepared to dislike you when you first arrived. I thought you'd be just another do-gooder, like my mother. And then when I saw you—the likeness was incredible! The golden hair and blue eyes . . .'

Charlotte laughed. 'Strange you should say that—I had a feeling we'd met before. Do you believe in reincarnation?'

'What a strange question! Probably not, but I agree with you about the feeling of togetherness. It's almost as if we'd been lovers before . . .'

'Or perhaps later,' she put in excitedly. How could she explain her feelings to him? 'I mean, supposing we don't marry in this life, we may meet up again in some far-off future . . .'

'Hey, steady on, Charlotte! You've lost me now.' Adam laughed nervously. 'We've got a great future ahead. You may look like my mother, but you're nothing like her in character.'

'I remember you told me she died when you were small.'

'She was killed in a plane crash in the Sahara. Her latest lover with with her.'

'I'm sorry.' Charlotte swallowed hard as she saw the look of resignation on his face.

'It doesn't hurt any more. It was all a long time ago. I never allow myself to dwell on the past. Only the present and the future concern me now.'

They were pulling into harbour. 'And where is your father?' she asked.

Adam took a deep breath. 'He committed suicide when my mother left us.'

She daren't speak; anything she said would sound trite. At last she understood him. She mustn't let him down.

They took a taxi around the coast of Hong Kong, and Charlotte marvelled at the beauty spread out before them, as they rounded each bend. The cloudless blue sky was reflected in the smooth sea as the car drove through the tiny village of Shek O and out to the end of the rocky promontory.

'There's the house!' Adam was pointing to an impressive stone building, high above a sandy cove. Tall trees shrouded its large garden, but the ornate roof was shining in the morning sunlight.

'It's beautiful!' breathed Charlotte.

The gates opened, as if by magic, as they approached. The servants had been watching the road for the past couple of hours, excited at the prospect of seeing their new master again. And he was not alone. There was a young lady with him. Did this mean . . .?

'Dr Forster, sir.' The white-coated steward held open the car door, glancing approvingly at the pretty companion.

'Hello, Sing Loong; this is Miss Craven.'

The servant bowed. 'Come this way, sir. We give you drinks.'

It was a full hour before they were able to escape by themselves. There were so many things for Adam to see to—the appointment of a new gardener, the colour of the new guest suite, the draining of the swimming pool so that they could fix the jacuzzi—it all took time, and he was longing to be alone with Charlotte. He wanted to get to the bottom of what was troubling her, once and for all.

When at last they ran hand in hand down the path to the beach, he felt a wonderful feeling of relief. He was glad there was no water in the pool; it was so much more romantic to swim out to one of the little islands . . .

He plunged into the warm sea and turned on to his back to check that Charlotte had followed. Her slim, lithe figure was only a couple of strokes behind him. He struck out towards the mound of rocks in the middle of the bay. No one would disturb them there.

He stretched himself out on the fine sand, an arm waiting to encircle her as she sank down beside him. For a few moments their lips joined in a sensual kiss, a lovers' kiss. Adam shivered and pulled himself away quickly.

'Let's talk, before I get carried away. First, do you like our house?'

'Adam, it's your house . . .'

'Do you like it?'

'I think it's fabulous, but . . .'

'I wanted somewhere to escape to if the pressures of running the refugee colony became too much. But now that I'm totally committed I'm going to see it through. It was Mai Ling who decided me. When I saw her that first day, abandoned on the beach . . .'

'What had happened to her?' Charlotte asked quietly.

'Pirates had boarded her ship; she was raped and thrown overboard, after her parents had been robbed and killed. When I first saw her, I knew I had to do something about the refugee problem. But I had to keep it secret, otherwise I would be creating a precedent that the authorities couldn't handle. All kinds of undesirable camps might have been set up and the problem would have got out of control . . . But we're not here to talk about my problems. What about yours? What's the trouble?'

'It's my heart,' she told him quietly. 'I've got a congenital malformation. The doctors think I've only about a year to live . . .'

'Oh, Charlotte, my poor, poor darling!' He pulled her into his arms and cradled her tightly against him as if fearing that at any moment she might be snatched from him. His mind was in utter turmoil by her awful revelation. He tried desperately to think clearly and objectively, but he was possessed by a feeling of panic. She mustn't die . . . he couldn't bear it! And she had been so brave . . . he would never have guessed that she had been under sentence of death. His breathing was laboured and stertorous as he attemped to become the analytical surgeon once more.

'Which doctors say you have a poor prognosis, my love?' he asked gently. He would leave no stone unturned, if there was the remotest chance that she could be saved.

'Some colleagues of my father. They were

concerned about my health after the deaths of my parents, so I underwent various tests, and it transpired that it was my heart.'

'But how do you know? Did they tell you so, in so many words?'

'Not exactly . . .'

'How do you mean, not exactly?' He sounded impatient at her evasive answers.

'I intercepted the result of my tests—not intentionally, of course,' Charlotte added hastily. 'I just happened to open the post in the surgery that morning, and there it was . . . Charlotte Craven, congenital malformation of the heart, surgery inadvisable, prognosis poor, about a year . . .' She reeled it off parrot fashion. The words had haunted her ever since she'd read them.

'But what are your symptoms?' asked Adam.

'At the moment I haven't any. I've never felt better in my life. Apart from the fact that my heart beats too quickly whenever you're around . . .'

'Don't be so unscientific!' He was laughing as he folded her in his arms and and covered her face with kissses. 'I refuse to take someone else's diagnosis. On the other hand, I'm too involved with you to make a rational judgement myself. We'd better have you admitted to St Margaret's as soon as possible. They'll run a series of tests on you, and then we can evaluate the findings. But I shall refuse to believe that it's inoperable.'

'I don't want surgery,' she said quietly. 'I don't want to lead the life of an invalid, depending on other people for everything I do, like my mother.'

'But it wouldn't be like that, Charlotte. Your mother was an older woman, not as strong as you. She probably had other complications. Surgery is advancing so fast nowadays; everything is possible!'

'I admire your optimism,' she whispered sadly, but her mind was made up.

'So what's your answer, my love?'

She gazed at him in disbelief. After all she'd said! 'To which question, Adam?

He smiled fondly. 'Will you marry me?'

'I can't!' It was an anguished cry, straight from the heart. 'I can't condemn you to stand by me. Leave me now, before we become any more involved with each other. It's impossible.'

'It's not impossible!' he cried angrily. 'I'll never give up. Whatever the outcome, you're mine.'

'No, no, no!' Charlotte was sobbing uncontrollably, holding her head in her hands, covering her ears so that she couldn't hear him.

'Listen to me!' He pulled her hands away roughly and held her to him again. 'We're in this together. I love you, Charlotte—I always will. Do you love me? Do you?'

'Yes, oh yes, I love you, Adam.' She was crying now, huge tears of frustration running down her cheeks, as she thought of what might have been.

He gently kissed away her salty tears, as he cradled her in his strong arms. 'Hush, little one; you're going to be all right.'

He lifted her in his arms and carried her back to the sea.

'It's OK, Adam; I can swim by myself. I swam out here, remember?'

But he was lowering her gently into the water, pulling her against his chest, as he swam on his back to the shore.

The next couple of hours passed in a haze of unreality. Charlotte heard Adam's voice on the telephone in the next room, as he organised the situation calmly.

'But Matron, I would like her to be admitted as soon as possible . . . Yes, of course I mean today.'

She lay very still, on the guest room bed, as she had been told to do. It was all out of her hands now. Adam had taken control of her life. It was up to him. She closed her eyes, feeling suddenly very tired.

When she awoke he was standing over her, looking down with an expression of indescribable tenderness. 'Time to go,' he whispered, lifting her off the bed.

It was useless to protest. He was determined to treat her like an invalid. She lay quietly in his arms as he carried her out to the waiting car.

The servants watched in silence. It was such a pity! They had no idea what was wrong with Dr Forster's girl-friend, but if anyone could cure her, he could. They'd heard about his reputation, long before he decided to buy the house. The young woman was in good hands.

Charlotte held tightly on to his hand as the car swept round the corners. 'Will you stay with me, Adam?' she asked softly, feeling scared at the prospect of losing him.

'I'll see you settled in, but then I'll have to

go back to Cheung Lau. I'll come back again tomorrow.' He dropped a gentle kiss on her cheek, and she smiled up at him, committing every rugged feature to memory, so that she could think of him in the night.

Matron O'Sullivan was waiting for them in the drive, in front of the hospital. Suddenly Charlotte realised she was a VIP! She was no longer the unqualified volunteer nurse, at everyone's beck and call. She was Dr Forster's fiancée! When she heard him describe her as such, she couldn't believe it. He was announcing their engagement to the whole of the medical fraternity, and she hadn't even said yes!

'You're incorrigible!' she whispered as he placed her on a stretcher.

'So are you. Just lie back and behave yourself. If you do everything you're told, we'll be able to set the wedding date.' He squeezed her hand and she smiled back. Perhaps she should go along with the charade. It couldn't do any harm . . .

Her room looked out over the Bay of Hong Kong. She would have liked to be in the open ward, but Adam wanted her to be alone.

'You need total rest and calm—besides, I want you to myself when I come to see you. The tests will start tomorrow. Don't look so worried! You've been through it all before and it didn't kill you. I'll come over as soon as I can.' He kissed her tenderly on the lips, and then he was gone.

Somehow Charlotte got through the night. Rather foolishly, she had rejected the offer of a sleeping pill. But she wanted to have time to herself, time to think about her future. She lay in the hard hospital bed, listening to the usual hospital sounds; the clang of an ambulance bell, the clanking of a trolley in the corridor, the loud snoring of a patient in the ward next door. But this time it was different. She was a patient now, not a nurse, and all the familiar sounds increased her tension. By the end of the week her worst suspicions would have been confirmed—and Adam would have changed his mind. He would have had time to reconsider his rash proposal. She was sure of it.

CHAPTER TEN

In the early hours of the morning Charlotte fell into a deep sleep, exhausted by her own thoughts and fears. She opened her eyes to find a charming Sister, in the familiar blue uniform that was used on Cheung Lau, smiling down at her.

'Where am I?' She was totally confused by her surroundings. What was she doing in a hospital bed? And this wasn't Cheung Lau. Then it all came flooding back, the events of the previous day.

'You've had a good sleep. I came in before, but you were fast asleep and it seemed a shame to waken you.' The Sister was shaking down the thermometer. 'I'll just take your TPR and then you can have a cup of tea. I'm Sister Ko, by the way.'

Charlotte observed the attractive Oriental features as she lay temporarily speechless with the thermometer under her tongue. How unusual for a Sister to be doing the TPR round, she thought, and then remembered that she was a VIP—Dr Forster's fiancée! Probably getting preferential treatment! She's taking a long time over my pulse rate, she thought.

Sister Ko examined the thermometer. 'Well, that looks perfectly normal. I'll just check your pulse again. I've forgotten what it was.' She gave an apologetic little laugh as she placed her fingers lightly on Charlotte's wrist.

'Is there something wrong?' Charlotte queried.

'Ah, that's for the doctors to decide,' was the ambiguous reply. Again, the same bright professional smile that gave nothing away. 'You've been placed in the care of Selwyn Grainger—*the* Selwyn Grainger.'

Charlotte looked blank. The name meant nothing to her.

'He's a famous cardiologist,' the Sister explained, remembering that Charlotte's knowledge of the medical fraternity, especially in this part of the world, was limited. 'Dr Forster has asked him to take charge of your case. He felt he was too involved to take charge of it himself.'

The colour rose to her cheeks. So everyone knew about her and Adam! She felt as if she were on a roller-coaster that was running away with her. It was like being in a dream, where you were trying to shout, 'Stop! I need time!' But life was sweeping her along relentlessly; no one was listening to her any more.

'What's happening to me today?' she asked, in a resigned tone.

'Let me see . . .' Sister Ko was consulting the case notes. Charlotte noted with a shiver of despair that they hadn't been left in her room. 'Here we are—screening for sepsis, routine blood tests, X-ray of chest and screening. Well, that will get some of the tests out of the way. And now a cup of tea, I think. You've got a bell by the side of the bed. Don't hesitate to ring if you need anything, will you?'

'Oh, but I'll be getting up as soon as I've drunk my tea . . .'

'Better not. Just to be on the safe side, we'd rather you stayed in bed. Until we've cleared all the tests, you understand. If you want to use the bathroom, ring the bell and someone will go with you.' The slim blue figure breezed out of the room.

Well, that's something, Charlotte thought; at least I don't have to use a bedpan! But the whole thing is preposterous! All these weeks I've been working flat out on Cheung Lau, and now I'm an invalid. It doesn't make sense. My UK report said I was to lead as normal a life as possible. I'll speak to Adam about it. A warm, sensual feeling flooded through her as she thought about him. Oh, Adam, I do so love you! I wish you were here with me now.

She giggled, almost upsetting her tea cup, as she had a mental picture of the eminent surgeon folding his long legs in the narrow bed beside her.

'That's what I like to see, a cheerful patient.' Charles Gordon swung into the room, unannounced.

'What a pleasant surprise!' Charlotte had only ever seen the anaesthetist over on Cheung Lau, when he was needed in theatre. 'I'd forgotten you were based over here. Is this a social call?'

'Yes and no.'

She laughed at his evasive answer. 'OK, give me the worst. You've come to take me down to theatre for a heart transplant?'

'Not exactly. First, the social bit. Congratulations, Charlotte! I think it's marvellous—you and Adam.' He was smiling all over his amiable face.

'News travels fast,' she remarked. 'Now, what about the professional bit?' she asked anxiously.

'Merely routine, my dear . . . just in case we have to take you down some time.' He was trying to sound casual, but she wasn't fooled as he approached the bed. 'Now, if I could listen to your chest . . .'

Sister Ko had returned to help the anaesthetist with his examination, a dazzlingly impersonal smile on her lips. 'Now, if you would turn this way . . .'

Charles Gordon straightened up and reached for the notes. 'Fine. You're doing very well, Charlotte. I'll see you later.' He scribbled something in the notes and made for the door.

There's something they're not telling me, she thought apprehensively, as the door swung shut. I can see it in their faces; the way they listen, and then listen again. The way they take my pulse twice. She felt for her wrist. Oh God, I'm becoming the perfect hypochondriac! It seems all right to me—but then I'm not an expert. Oh, Adam, what are you doing to me? Just when I'd resigned myself to the future, you come along to upset all my resolutions. But where are you, now that I need you?

She turned over on her side and began to sob into the pillow.

'My goodness me, we can't have this!' Matron O'Sullivan strode into the room and hurried towards the bed. 'My poor child, it's all been too much for you, hasn't it . . . getting engaged, and coming into hospital . . .'

Charlotte lifted her head off the pillow and reached for a tissue. The old dear was more perceptive than she had thought! She smiled up into the kindly face. 'I'm sorry, Matron,' she sniffed.

'Sorry? There's no need to be sorry, my dear. You have a good cry if you feel like it. But it does seem a shame when you've got so much to be thankful for. I mean, all the unattached girls in this hospital would give their eye teeth to be engaged to Dr Forster. And don't look at me like that! I know what I'm talking about. I like to keep my ear to the ground. Why, Dr Forster! We were just talking about you.'

'Adam!' Charlotte held out her arms in an automatic gesture of welcome, as the handsome figure walked through the door.

Kate O'Sullivan gave a nervous cough. Time for her to make a hasty retreat and allow the lovers some time together. This would cure the girl's weepies! 'Nice to see you again, Adam. I'm afraid I must dash . . . if there's anything I can do . . .' The starched white cap on the grey curls shook precariously as she made her escape.

They were alone. It took three long strides for Adam to reach the bed. He folded Charlotte into his arms, covering her face with kisses, before his lips settled on hers in a long, blissful union.

'I've missed you so much, Adam. I couldn't wait to see you again.'

'I came as soon as I could—well, almost as soon.' He was smiling sheepishly.

'What do you mean?'

'I made a little detour on my way here. I stopped off at the jewellers.' From the pocket of his dark tailored suit he was pulling a small square velvet box. 'I hope you like it.'

She gazed at the huge solitaire diamond set in an antique gold setting. 'Is that for me?' she asked incredulously.

He laughed. 'Well, it's certainly not for Matron! Try it on.' He was lifting it from the silken interior of the box. It shone and sparkled in the bright morning sunlight that flooded the room. He placed his hand over hers. 'With this ring . . .'

'Don't, Adam! It's unlucky to joke about something like that.' Charlotte's eyes filled with tears as she looked up into the face of the man she would so like to marry . . . if only . . .

'I'm sorry, darling.' He was threading the ring on to her finger.

It was much too big. 'Hardly the perfect fit!' he said, laughing lightly. 'I didn't realise you had such slim fingers. They told me at the shop that this was an average fitting; but then I forgot, you're not average, you're very special . . .'

He held her very close, parting her lips with his own. The ring fell from her finger and they both scrabbled among the sheets trying to find it.

'Here it is!' he grinned triumphantly as he placed the ring on the tip of his little finger. 'Well, it fits me, but I suppose I'd better take it back. They said if it was the wrong size to tie a piece of cotton round your finger, like this . . . and they'll have it made smaller for you.'

Charlotte watched him slip the box into his pocket, wondering how long she would wear the ring. Her attention was claimed by the arrival of the consultant.

'Selwyn! I'm glad you're here. This is my fiancée, Charlotte Craven . . .' Adam introduced her.

'I believe we met briefly at the Frobishers'

dinner party.' The tall distinguished figure walked over to the bed.

'Yes, of course; I remember you now, Dr Grainger.' She looked up into the calm brown eyes of the cardiologist. His brown hair was greying at the temples. He looked about mid-forties, and he exuded an air of confidence. She felt safe with a man like this in charge—especially if Adam approved.

He sat down on the bed, smiling at the rumpled sheets.

'We were only looking for my engagement ring.' Her cheeks had flushed a pretty pink.

Adam laughed. 'I wouldn't dream of upsetting your patient, Selwyn.'

'Of course not.' The cardiologist patted her hand. 'Now, let's find out something about you. I've had a look at your case history, but if you could fill me in on a few relevant details . . .'

Charlotte repeated her story; the startling revelation that she had only a year to live . . .

A young medical secretary had made her discreet entrance and taken notes of the proceedings. 'I'll have these typed up for you, sir,' she said, as she went out.

He nodded briefly, and turned back to his patient. 'If there's anything else you think I should know . . .'

Charlotte was tired of the interrogation, and longing for him to leave her alone with Adam. She had seen him glancing at his watch and knew that time was short. Any minute now he would announce that he had to be getting back to the hospital on Cheung Lau. 'I'm sure you've got all the details you need,' she said.

He stood up and held out his hand. 'We'll

keep you informed of our findings,' he assured her.

She watched him go, with a sense of relief, but as he went he passed another doctor on his way in.

'I have to screen you for sepsis,' the young man told Charlotte importantly. 'Ah, Dr Forster, I hadn't seen you there. Shall I come back?'

'No, that's OK, John. Carry on. I've got to go. This is Dr Brett, Charlotte.'

She nodded her head, a resigned smile on her lips. Adam was preparing to leave her. She felt in a panic! 'When shall I see you again?' she asked anxiously.

'Tomorrow,' he replied, in a matter-of-fact voice.

Tomorrow! That was a lifetime away! 'I wish you didn't have to go.' She sounded like a little child.

'So do I.' His voice was husky with sincerity as he leaned across to brush his lips over hers. 'But duty calls. Don't worry, my love. You're in good hands.'

So everyone keeps telling me, she thought. She watched miserably as Adam left her, turning at the door to blow a kiss.

Perhaps I shouldn't have barged in like this, thought John Brett. She must be extremely important to rate the sort of treatment she's getting. Fancy sending for a doctor to take a routine throat swab, not to mention the nasal tip swab!

'Open your mouth wide, Miss Craven. That's fine . . .'

Charlotte suffered the indignities bestowed upon her by the young doctor, her mind still with Adam. She wondered if he had left the hospital, or if he'd stopped to confer with Dr Grainger about her case.

'And now we need some blood for our various tests. Would you roll up your sleeve, please?'

She complied, as if in a trance. Her body no longer belonged to her. She didn't feel a thing as the needle entered her vein.

'Well, that's a good rich colour!' John Brett was smiling at his little joke.

Charlotte smiled back politely, wishing he would go.

'Time for your chest X-ray, Miss Craven.' Sister swept into the room. 'Oh, will you be long, Dr Brett?'

'Just finished, Sister.'

'I haven't had any breakfast yet.' She'd had enough for one morning, and felt faint from hunger.

'I'm so sorry—we forgot all about you in the confusion. Well, I mean, everyone came at once. What would you like?' Sister asked apologetically.

'Just toast and coffee, please. Is there time before my X-ray?'

'Of course.' Sister sounded surprised at the question. All she would have to do was make a phone call. She couldn't inconvenience Dr Forster's fiancée, now, could she?

As Charlotte drank her coffee slowly, the bedside phone rang. It was Adam! At the sound of his voice her heart leapt for joy.

'Where are you?' she asked.

'I'm still in the hospital. I called in to see Selwyn.'

'I thought you would.'

'We're both agreed that it would be a good

idea to get in touch with the hospital where you had your last set of tests. Where was it?'

She told him, her heart thumping madly. 'Why do you want to contact them, Adam? I thought you wanted to make your own decision.'

'Purely routine, darling. In the end, it will be our own findings that count. Are you OK? You sound a bit . . .'

'I'm fine,' she said brightly.

'That's my girl! I'll see you tomorrow. Goodbye.'

Charlotte stared into the phone, willing herself to see the rugged features and sensual mouth. Will I ever get through the day without him? she wondered.

Sister appeared, pushing a chair. 'I thought you would prefer this to a stretcher. So, if you're ready for our little jaunt . . .'

She hadn't realised how beautiful the hospital was. Set right on the Peak, it commanded the most mind-blowing views of the Bay of Hong Kong.

'Sister, can we stop for a moment?' she cried, as they went along an outside verandah, high above the fabulous city.

Sister Ko smiled. 'I'd forgotten you'd never been here before. It's very impressive, isn't it?'

'It's out of this world!' Charlotte could see the boats on the water, moving endlessly between Hong Kong and Kowloon, the huge ocean-going liners tied up in Victoria Harbour and the continual streams of traffic snaking up and down the Peak road. 'The patients are very lucky to be in a place like this.' She smiled at her own enthusiasm. For a few seconds she had forgotten that she was a patient; forgotten that there was a shadow hanging over her otherwise blissful life . . .

'Have you seen enough? Shall we go now?'

'Yes, let's go, Sister.'

Sister Ko pushed the chair, wondering why her patient had become so subdued again. These sudden swings of mood were very strange. I'll have to mention it to Dr Grainger, she was thinking.

There was barely time to get back into bed after her X-rays before Charlotte had to set off again for an electrocardiogram. By early afternoon she was feeling that if she had to take another test that day she would scream! It was all very well telling her she must rest—she just wished she had the opportunity!

The door was pushed slightly open. 'I thought you might be asleep,' said a voice.

'Jane! How lovely to see you. Asleep? You must be joking! They're putting me through every kind of known torture. I felt marvellous before I came in—now I feel dreadful!'

Jane laughed. 'You poor thing! I was so worried when Mark told me about you. But I'm thrilled about the engagement. What a dark horse you are! You might have given me a little hint of what was going on.'

'Honestly, Jane, I didn't know myself until a couple of days ago . . .'

'Oh, pull the other one! But seriously, what about your health? Why didn't you say something when you first arrived? I knew you had a problem. I said to Mark . . .'

'I didn't want anyone to know,' Charlotte explained. 'I wanted to lead a normal life—and I succeeded. I had all those weeks on Cheung Lau in the hospital. Look at me now! Stuck here in a hospital bed . . .'

'But it won't be for long. As soon as they've finished the tests you'll be able . . .'

'Yes?' She knew that Jane had been going to say that she would be able to be discharged, but that wasn't the case at all, and they both knew it. If the UK diagnosis was confirmed, Adam would start thinking in terms of surgery.

Jane reached out and squeezed her friend's hand. 'Don't worry,' she said, knowing that her platitudes were inadequate. 'So when's the great day, then?'

Charlotte frowned, and Jane misinterpreted her puzzled look. 'The wedding! When are you getting married?'

'It will depend . . .'

'On what?'

'On the tests, for God's sake!'

'Sorry—I only asked,' said Jane rather huffily.

'And I'm sorry, Jane. I didn't mean to shout at you.'

'No, of course you didn't. You're having a tough time in here.' Jane stood up.

'You're not going, are you?' asked Charlotte.

'Afraid so. This is just a flying visit. I've got to meet Mark downstairs in a couple of minutes— but I'll come back tomorrow.'

If only tomorrow would come! thought Charlotte, as she watched her friend disappear through the door.

Adam phoned during the evening. He sounded tired. It was bad news about the refugee colony. The police had been making enquiries—headed by Sargeant Leung, of course! 'If we don't get the legal situation sorted out within the next few days, they'll all be carted off to the mainland, and I'll be for the high jump!' he said in a worried voice. 'But I mustn't upset you, Charlotte. It's my problem. How's your day gone?'

'Rather like the Inquisition.' She tried to sound as if it was all a great big joke.

'You're a brave girl. Keep your chin up. It's worth going through this, so that we can have peace of mind. I'll be in to see you tomorrow—I don't know when, but I'll make it. Goodnight, darling.'

The next day was very similar, except that she wasn't allowed breakfast.

'You're going down for a cardiac catheterisation, and there's a possibility you may have a general anaesthetic,' Sister said brightly. She had already told Charles Gordon that she thought Charlotte would be difficult to handle without an anaesthetic, but it would be up to Dr Grainger to make the decision.

'I don't think a general is necessary,' boomed the great man, staring down at Adam Forster's fiancée, as she lay in the ante-room, under the bright lights. No, she looked a plucky little thing. 'You're not nervous, my dear, are you?'

'Well . . .' Charlotte began.

'No, of course you're not. Probably enjoy watching the proceedings!'

Her tummy was definitely rumbling. A cup of coffee would have been nice . . . but they were approaching her again. Oh, why wasn't Adam there? He'd said he would come over and she so wanted to see him again.

'We'll give you a sedative and a local anaesthetic,' said the deep voice above her.

She nodded apprehensively. Perhaps she should insist on a general anaesthetic? They didn't know what a coward she was. Too late!

'And then I'm going to introduce a radio-paque catheter into the antecubital vein, in front of the elbow.'

She was being wheeled into a darkened room and the voice was going with her, giving a running commentary. She felt as if the whole thing were happening to someone else.

'By using fluoroscopy, the tip of the catheter can be seen entering the right atrium, ventricle and pulmonary artery, and any abnormal communications can be demonstrated . . .'

I shall probably die of fright, Charlotte thought. That would save them all a lot of trouble. She closed her eyes and held her breath. The ordeal seemed endless.

They were wheeling her back to her room. 'There, that wasn't too bad, was it?'

She smiled up at the relief Sister, enjoying the sound of the lilting Welsh accent. Jane had told her that Wendy Jones had a heart of gold and was brilliant at her job. She was prepared to like the fair-haired young woman. 'I wouldn't want to go through it again today,' she confessed.

Sister Jones laughed. 'No, of course you wouldn't, and I don't blame you. There's a limit to these endurance tests, isn't there—oh, Dr Forster rang while you were down.' Charlotte's heart began to beat faster. 'Said he's been held up, but he'll try and get over later on.'

Was it trouble with the refugees? she wondered. Or was it the hospital? She felt so useless, as she was helped back into bed. Just when he needs me, I'm lying here, of no use to anyone, she thought unhappily.

'How many more tests do I have to undergo, Sister?' she asked.

'Well, let's have a look, shall we? Oh, the notes are in the office, aren't they?'

Yes, they most certainly are, thought Charlotte grimly. Otherwise I would have found out for myself. She watched the pretty little Sister returning, clutching the precious file. 'Not much more, I'm glad to say. We need a clinical estimate of your respiratory efficiency—that'll be done tomorrow—and an echocardiograph, probably the day after. That's about it, so don't look so glum. I expect you're dying to get on with your wedding plans. Jane told me all about it . . .'

Charlotte fended off the questions, pleading that she was tired. Wendy Jones went away with the distinct idea that her patient had mixed feelings about the wedding, but she wasn't going to voice her opinion to anyone, least of all her friend Jane, who was in raptures over the whole thing.

When the phone rang, minutes later, Charlotte grabbed it eagerly. 'Darling, where are you?' she asked.

Adam sounded weary and disillusioned. 'I'm at police headquarters . . . Don't worry; my lawyer is due to arrive soon, and he'll sort things out. But I can't get away tonight. I'll phone you tomorrow . . . can't talk now.'

There was a click, and the phone went dead. Charlotte blinked back her tears. It was all such a mess! Everything was going wrong, just at the time when she should have been on top of the world, getting ready for a wedding. It seemed even more unlikely, now.

When he rang again, next morning, she was resigned for the worst. Yes, she understood perfectly. No, he mustn't think of leaving in the middle of the refugee case.

'You've got to see it through now, Adam. It's what you've been fighting for . . . Yes, I'm fine . . . I'm only having a few potty little tests, for God's sake! It's not major surgery.' She even managed a little laugh, but her spirits sank to rock bottom, as she replaced the phone.

She couldn't remember what day it was . . . as if it mattered, anyway! They were all the same in here. She found she was sleeping more and more, in the daytime, when she wasn't being jabbed or prodded or listened to. She could have read one of the books Jane had brought in for her, but it was too much effort . . .

The days passed. Jenny Benson called in one afternoon, and she welcomed the new face.

'You poor little poppet,' she said, strewing the bed with an enormous bunch of roses and chrysanthemums. 'I was devastated when they told me. How are you feeling?'

'I'm OK. Have you seen Adam?'

Jenny regarded her warily. She had been told she mustn't discuss the refugee case. It was all very hush-hush. She mustn't put her foot in it. 'I saw him this morning.'

'How is he?'

'He's fine.' No point in telling the poor girl that the strain was beginning to show. She'd got enough to worry about.

'Thank you for the flowers.' Charlotte was dying to ask about Mai Ling, Wing Tai, Yin

Fen . . . but she daren't. Instead they made polite conversation for a few minutes, before Jenny glanced at her watch.

'Good heavens, is that the time? I've got an appointment.'

They were both relieved the ordeal was over. Jenny left, promising to visit again soon. When she had gone, Charlotte turned over and went back to sleep. She had ceased to dream. There was only a deep black, welcome void.

Someone was standing over her. She must be dreaming again. It was Adam! He looked thinner, and utterly weary, but his strong features were still handsome. Her heart still fluttered madly at the sight of him. She reached up and her arms encountered real flesh and blood.

'Darling, I've missed you so much!' she sighed.

'I couldn't get here before. They're still deciding the fate of the refugees, but I had to come and see you. Selwyn Grainger phoned me . . .'

'And . . .?' Charlotte held her breath.

'We've just had a long conference.'

'So you've got the results of all my tests?'

'Yes.' Adam's face was serious. He pulled her close to him, kissing her gently on the lips.

She gazed up into his eyes. 'Tell me, Adam. I want to know what's wrong with me.'

CHAPTER ELEVEN

ADAM took her hand firmly in his own as he made himself comfortable on the edge of the bed.

'I'll make it as simple as I can. All the tests show that you have no heart tissue disease . . .'

Charlotte gave a sigh of relief.

'. . . *but*—there *is* a pathological abnormality.'

Cold muscles gripped at her heart. 'What does that mean? What kind of abnormality?' Even as she asked the questions, she didn't want him to tell her. She didn't want him to confirm her worst fears and shatter the last of her dreams.

'It's not as bad as you think.'

Oh no! Let's look on the bright side, at all costs!

'You have an extra heartbeat. Every third beat goes dub *dub* dub instead of dub dub.'

She stared at him. 'Is this serious? I mean, can it be cured?' Oh, she did so want to live!

'If you'd come to me ten years ago, I would have been rather gloomy, but recent research has proved that this sort of abnormality is not dangerous, provided that there's no evidence of diseased tissue or other complications. In your case, you can more or less ignore it. I'll keep an eye on you and we'll run periodic checks over the years . . .'

'You mean you still want to marry me?' Charlotte was so confused by the revelation.

'What a stupid question!' Adam was laughing at the sight of her puzzled face. 'Of course I want to marry you. I've just told you, you can lead a normal life.'

'That's what the UK report said,' she put in quietly.

A shadow crossed his face. 'I'm still trying to get an answer from them. The consultant in charge of your case has moved and his successor is searching the records. They've promised to send me a full report. I told them it was urgent, but there must have been a snarl-up in the communications.' He was trying to sound lighthearted, but at the back of his mind there was still a tiny doubt. Was it possible that they had found something that his team had missed?

'I feel like a circus freak,' Charlotte said softly.

He smiled down at her intense little face. 'You're not a freak, you're someone very special. Not everyone has an amazing heart like yours. I might even ask you to help me out in teaching sessions with my students . . .'

'You brute!' She pulled her hand away from his, laughing gaily for the first time in days.

'You can't escape so easily.' Adam pulled her roughly back into his arms.

When Sister Jones walked in, she was witness to the fact that the wedding was most definitely on again! 'Oh, I'm sorry, sir,' she apologised. 'I didn't know you were in here.'

'That's OK, Sister. We're just going.' He got up off the bed.

'*We*'re going?' Charlotte had begun to feel she was a permanent fixture of the hospital.

'Of course. Unless you prefer to spend another night here?' He smiled down at her.

'You must be joking!' She was pulling back the covers.

'I'll get your clothes,' said Wendy Jones laughingly. It was good to see her patient looking so happy again. 'And I shall expect an invitation to the wedding.'

'You're already on our list,' Adam replied. 'Jane's been working on it all week.'

'Well, I think I'll take over from her now,' Charlotte said firmly. She knew Jane had only the best intentions, but she'd had enough of being taken care of. From now on, she was in charge.

They sailed back over the water in the sunset. The rays of the dying sun were the same colour as her catsuit. She glanced down at it, remembering how she had chosen it with care, all those days ago. It seemed like a lifetime since they had sailed out of Cheung Lau harbour. And now the sentence of death had been removed—thanks to Adam. She glanced up at the confident face of the man she loved so much. They had a lifetime together ahead of them. Whatever happened to her, Adam would be by her side. Her fingers tightened automatically on his.

'Happy?' he asked, smiling at her rapturous expression.

She nodded. Her heart was too full for words.

The sun had set by the time Jim manoeuvred the boat against the jetty. The evening lights twinkled along the water's edge. The stallholders were still intent on selling their wares, as they passed through the little town, hand in hand.

'There goes the doctor—and that's the girl he's going to marry.' 'She's been very ill, in hospital, I hear.' 'Yes, but he's cured' her.' 'Miraculous, isn't it? When's the wedding?'

Charlotte smiled at the friendly faces, enjoying the sound of their lilting voices. I wonder if they're talking about us, she was thinking. They seem more than usually interested . . .

Sister Benson was sitting at her desk in Reception, finishing her day report. She put down her pen and hurried over to meet the happy couple.

'Congratulations!—on both sets of news. Dr Grainger phoned me to report on your health, and . . . well, what can I say about the wedding? It's wonderful . . . like a fairy tale!' She looked as if she was going to weep.

'With a happy ending,' Adam put in quietly, squeezing Charlotte's hand.

'I've been along to see that your room's ready. I expect you'll want to get to bed—*Charlotte*,' she added quickly, hoping that they wouldn't misinterpret her words. She hadn't meant . . .

Adam laughed. 'I'll see the patient to her room. Good night.'

They were alone at last. Charlotte's little room had never looked so inviting. Helen Benson had filled it with fresh flowers, and turned on the bedside lamp. She threw herself on the bed and gave a sigh of relief.

'I don't know why I should feel so tired—I've done nothing for the past few days. Do you think I could go back on duty tomorrow? I've got withdrawal symptoms from work.'

Adam laughed. 'I think you should let yourself in gently. It's been quite an ordeal for you. And then there's going to be all the preparation for the wedding. I thought you might like to have a hand in getting our house ready . . .'

'You mean, the house at Shek O?' She remembered the fabulous building on the edge of the sea, with its luxurious furniture, its rich damask curtains and thick carpets. She was to be Mrs Adam Forster, mistress of this wonderful home!

'You do like the place, don't you?' he asked anxiously.

'I love it,' she breathed. 'But not as much as I love you.'

He took her in his arms, with a new gentleness, as if she were made of Dresden china. But the contact with her body was too much for him. His pulses began to race. She was clinging to him passionately wanting him as much as he wanted her . . .

Charlotte stirred in Adam's arms. Outside there was the sound of an owl hooting. She glanced at her watch. It was very late! How long had they been asleep? She lay quietly watching the moon, high above the trees, a strange sense of peace stealing over her. This was where she belonged— in Adam's arms, for ever.

He opened his eyes and stared at her fondly, as if unable to believe that she was actually there.

'You'd better go, Adam,' she said softly.

He grinned. 'Why?'

'Someone might phone your room or something,' she answered lamely.

'Well, they'd know where to find me if they got no reply,' he said mischievously.

'That's what I'm afraid of . . .'

'Oh, don't be such a prude!' he laughed. 'We're going to be married, remember? Which reminds me—your ring.' He sat up and reached for his jacket. Charlotte watched with bated breath as he took out the velvet box. 'I hope it fits this time.' He took her left hand in his and slid the slim gold band on her finger.

'It's perfect!' She stared down at the shining diamond.

'Good; because I've ordered the wedding ring that matches it in the same size. I hope you don't mind?'

'I love it.' She enjoyed Adam's masterful ways.

He kissed her gently. 'I'm going now; I wouldn't want your reputation tarnished before I've time to make an honest woman of you!'

She smiled happily, as she watched him tiptoe out on to the verandah. The moon put dancing highlights into his tousled fair hair. She remembered what the fortune-teller had tried to tell her. 'You will have three golden-haired sons'. It was not so improbable as she had thought.

It was impossible to sleep next morning. At the first dawn of the sun's rays, she was wide awake and raring to go. She took a quick shower and put on the crisply laundered white uniform. It was good to be back!

Sister Chen was amazed to find her helping the night staff with beds, when she arrived on duty.

'Nurse Craven, I hadn't expected to see you here this morning. No one told me you were returning.' Her shrewd eyes were glancing down at the girl's ring finger. Engagement rings were forbidden on duty, for reasons of hygiene. She was glad to see that Charlotte's hand was ringless. The girl had more sense than she gave her credit for.

'I wanted to get back on duty, Sister. If you don't need me here . . .'

'Oh, we can always do with an extra pair of hands, Nurse.' Sister cleared her throat, wondering what she should say about the news that had been the talk of the hospital all week. 'I believe congratulations are in order.'

Charlotte looked startled. She glanced apprehensively at the older woman, expecting to hear some caustic comment.

'I hope you'll both be very happy.' There, she'd said it, and it had been quite painless! Sister Chen smiled as she saw the pleasure her words had given to the young nurse.

'Perhaps you'd like to hear the night nurse's report with me, as you've been away so long. It would help you to get back into the swing of things.'

'I'd like that very much!' Charlotte was being treated like a trained nurse at last!

She joined Sister at her desk, and listened with interest to the long report. Mr Chang, the broncho-pneumonia, could go home today, if his X-rays were clear, but he must be warned about the dangers of smoking . . .

Charlotte suppressed a smile, wondering who would volunteer to press home the information. Her smile broadened as she watched the doors open. Adam was wearing his white coat, his stethoscope hung loosely around his neck, and everything was exactly as it had been before she went away.

He returned her welcoming smile. So this was where she had been hiding! Well, it was as safe a place as any; couldn't come to much harm in hospital, but he would prefer to keep an eye on her until he'd had the UK report . . . just in case. 'Sorry to disturb your report, Sister; I wonder if I might borrow Nurse Craven for the day?' he said.

Sister Chen screwed up her Oriental features, as if she were considering his request. 'I think that might be arranged, Doctor,' she said solemnly.

Charlotte blushed. Whatever was he up to now? 'Thank you, Sister.' She hurried over to the door.

Adam kissed her as the doors swung to. 'Good morning, darling. Did you sleep well?'

'Yes, I did,' she replied breathlessly. 'Where are you taking me?'

'First to Obstetrics to check on my patients . . .' He was propelling her along the corridor. 'You haven't yet met the youngest member of the Pang family, have you? This is Adam Pang.'

Charlotte stared down at the tiny baby in his mother's arms, stifling a smile at the name.

'Mrs Pang asked if she could call him after me.' He had noticed her amusement. 'I think there must be more Adams in this part of the world than anywhere else!'

'I was hoping to use the name myself,' Charlotte put in softly.

'Oh, I think that could be arranged,' he replied, and their eyes met above the patient's head.

Mrs Pang noticed the conspiratorial glance, and smiled to herself. Nurse Lee had told her about the forthcoming wedding. It couldn't have happened to a nicer couple, she thought. They look so much in love. I hope they have as many sons as I have.

She repeated her thoughts out loud in Cantonese, and Adam smiled.

'She hopes we have three sons,' he said.

'I hope so, too.' Charlotte's eyes shone with happiness. There must be something about the number three. 'May I hold him for a moment?'

Mrs Pang handed over the tiny baby, who slept on undisturbed, now that his hunger had been appeased. Charlotte waited for Adam to finish his round of the patients before handing back the precious bundle.

He took her hand as they left the ward. 'We're going over to see Mai Ling,' he announced excitedly. 'I've just heard from my lawyer. He's swung the case in my favour. The refugees can stay—subject to various conditions, of course.'

'Oh, Adam, I'm so glad!' Charlotte reached up to pull his head down so that their lips could meet.

'And I'm so relieved!' He held her at arm's length. Only one tiny cloud on the horizon now. 'Let's go and tell Sister Benson where we're going. I've asked Charles to come over for the day. He should be here soon.'

The horse picked its way carefully up the steep hillside path. Charlotte had offered to try and ride one of the ponies in the hospital stable, but Adam had demurred.

'I like the feel of your arms around my waist,' he had told her, with a mischievous grin.

She wasn't sorry to cling on to him. She felt very safe. They rode into the camp as the children came rushing out to greet them. Wing Tai was wearing the new prosthesis on his leg and had dispensed entirely with his crutches, in favour of a walking stick. Yin Fen had trouble keeping up with her friend as she hurried out to see the doctor and nurse arriving on horseback.

'Where's Mai Ling?' asked Adam, when they had finished their protracted greetings.

'I'm here.' The young mother came shyly towards them, carrying her baby on her hip.

'Gather your things together, Mai Ling. You're leaving today.'

Her eyes widened in disbelief. She had come to think that all the discussion about a new life in Australia had meant nothing to the kind lady who had befriended her. Was it possible that her dreams were to come true after all?

'Jenny wants to leave on this evening's plane,' Adam told her. 'I'll send someone for you this afternoon. Can you be ready?'

She nodded excitedly. Of course she would be ready. She had nothing to pack—only a few things for the baby.

Wing Tai was showing off his ability to walk on the new limb, and Charlotte clapped her hands in delight. 'Isn't he clever, Adam?' She lowered her voice. 'What's going to happen to him now?'

'I'm going to expand the medical facilities; bring in a full-time physiotherapist, make a road between here and the hospital so that we can be in constant communication.'

'But when he's fully recovered . . .?'

'I'm trying, all the time, to find good homes

for the children. I've got world-wide contacts. Now that the project is legal, we can make real progress.'

She looked up into his shining eyes, loving his boyish enthusiasm. She would help him all she could with his plans. It would be a lifetime's commitment.

They made their way back over the hill, pausing at the summit to take in the superb view of the harbour, bustling with activity in the morning sunlight. 'Will you come to the airport with me this evening?' Adam asked quietly.

'Of course.' She wanted to go everywhere with him. There must be no further partings.

Nurse Lee came running out of the hospital to greet them. 'This letter came for you, Dr Forster. It's marked urgent, so I thought . . .'

Adam leapt down from the horse, lifting Charlotte swiftly down beside him. The stable boy came out to take over.

It was a UK postmark; Adam's fingers trembled as he slit open the envelope. His brow creased into a frown as he read on.

'Adam, what is it?' She was frightened. 'Is it my report?'

He nodded. 'Come inside, and I'll explain.'

A cold shiver ran down her spine as he squeezed her hand and led her along to his room. She sat down in one of the deep armchairs, her eyes on his solemn face.

'There's been a serious mistake,' he began. 'A million-to-one chance. Apparently the report you read was not meant for you.'

'But it had my name on it . . .'

'That's what I mean by a million-to-one chance. There is another Charlotte Craven—or rather, there was. She died last week, at the age of seventy-three. If you'd read the whole of the report, you would have seen the age discrepancy.'

'But I don't understand. Why was it sent to me?'

He put an arm round her shoulder. 'It was a clerical error. A temporary typist looked up Charlotte Craven's address and sent it to you. She sent your report to the other patient's doctor. He realised he'd got the wrong report, sent it back and got the correct one. But, as no one had complained about an erroneous report from your surgery, and the temporary typist had left by then, it was assumed that she had omitted to send off your report. A correct report has been waiting for you, with your father's partner. Their findings are exactly the same as ours.'

'So that was why the other Charlotte Craven couldn't undergo surgery! She had other complications, I suppose.' It was almost too much to take in all at once. Charlotte had lived for so long with the fateful words engraved on her memory.

'Her general health was poor, and she had senile dementia—not a suitable candidate for open heart surgery. I believe she died peacefully, if that's any consolation to you. I gather it was a blessing.'

'If only I hadn't opened that report!' sighed Charlotte. 'I feel such a fool!'

'I'm glad you did open it—otherwise we might never have met,' Adam said quietly.

'I never thought of that.' A great weight had been lifted from her. At last she was free of all nagging fears. Adam would take care of her heart for the rest of her life.

He was experiencing the same feeling of relief. There wasn't a cloud on the horizon! 'So now that we've cleared that up, I hope you'll be able to give your mind to the wedding plans, Mrs Forster.'

'What had you in mind, Doctor?' she asked softly.

'Well, for a start, you haven't kissed me for at least half an hour!'

Loving

Little Heather Fraser had everything she could
possibly want, except the love of her father, Jay.

His callousness shocked the tiny Cotswold village,
and most of all Claire Richards, whose daughter Lucy
was Heather's friend.

When Jay accused Claire of encouraging the girls'
friendship so that she could see more of *him*, nothing
could have been further from the truth.

A freak accident suddenly put paid to Claire's
cherished independence. Would she be able to swallow
her angry pride and reluctantly share the Frasers'
roof?

After 25 million sales worldwide, best-selling
author Penny Jordan presents her 50th Mills & Boon
romance for you to enjoy.

Available January 1987
Price £1.50.

Doctor Nurse Romances

Romance in modern medical life

Read more about the lives and loves of doctors and nurses in the fascinatingly different backgrounds of contemporary medicine. These are the three Doctor Nurse romances to look out for next month.

A SURGEON AT ST MARK'S
Elizabeth Harrison

NO ORDINARY NURSE
Sarah Franklin

A CASE FOR SPECIAL CARE
Judith Worthy

Buy them from your usual paperback stockist, or write to: Mills & Boon Reader Service, P.O. Box 236, Thornton Rd, Croydon, Surrey CR9 3RU, England. Readers in Southern Africa — write to: Independent Book Services Pty, Postbag X3010, Randburg, 2125, S. Africa.

Mills & Boon
the rose of romance

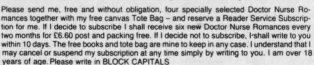